JOURNEY *of* FAITH:

Catholic Marriage Preparation

JOURNEY *of* FAITH:

Catholic Marriage Preparation

Deacon Roy Barkley, Ph.D.

Queenship

PUBLISHING COMPANY
P.O. Box 220 • Goleta, CA 93116
(800) 647-9882 • (805) 692-0043 • Fax: (805) 967-55133

JOURNEY OF FAITH:
CATHOLIC MARRIAGE PREPARATION

Deacon Roy Barkley, Ph.D.

The very preparation for Christian marriage is itself a journey of faith. It is a special opportunity for the engaged to rediscover and deepen the faith received in Baptism and nourished by their Christian upbringing. In this way they come to recognize and freely accept their vocation to follow Christ and to serve the Kingdom of God in the married state.

Pope John Paul II

Library of Congress Number: 02-141051

Published by:
    Queenship Publishing
    P.O. Box 220
    Goleta, CA 93116
    (800) 647-9882 • (805) 692-0043 • Fax: (805) 967-5133
    http://www.queenship.org

Printed in the United States of America

ISBN: 1-57918-179-1

CONTENTS

Dedication: To the Readers   Page VII

1. Looking Ahead: Invitation to Catholic Marriage   Page 1

2. Beginning Preparation   Page 13

3. Marriage as a Sacrament and Vocation   Page 25

4. Sexuality   Page 35

5. Children   Page 45

6. Models of the Family   Page 57

7. Family Dynamics   Page 67

8. Money and Possessions   Page 85

9. Planning Your Ceremony   Page 93

Sources and Suggestions for Further Reading   Page 109

Prefatory Note and Acknowledgements

I want to express my thanks here to Randy and Nancy McCaslin, directors of Natural Family Planning for Central Texas, for reading the first draft of this book and making valuable suggestions. I have been privileged to share in their mission for several rewarding years. Dr. Mary Shivanandan, of the Pope John Paul II Institute on Marriage and Family in Washington, D.C., also read the manuscript and gave excellent advice. I thank her.

I also thank the couples to whom this book is dedicated, both those whom I have helped prepare for marriage and those who will read this book. Their wellbeing is the purpose of the book and the goal of my prayers.

Quotations from Scripture in the first eight chapters are from the Revised Standard Version. Quotations for reading in weddings, in Chapter 9, are from the Lectionary.

DEDICATION: TO THE READERS

This book is dedicated to its users—engaged couples who come to the Catholic Church to prepare for the sacrament of Matrimony. It is written with the assumption that most who approach the Church for this great sacrament do so in a spirit of inquiry and obedience to the teachings of Christ. I know from experience, however, that some couples don't take the preparation very seriously. Some look upon it as a mere hurdle—an obstacle that they have to get past before they can proceed. They think it's sort of like passing a driving test or a physical exam: get through it, and then you can relax and do as you please. If you are like that, this book is very much for you. I offer it with a prayer that you will receive the teaching of the Church in your hearts and live by this teaching to the best of your ability. For Christ is the way to a full and blessed life.

No matter what their education and experience may be, people who come to the Church for marriage preparation usually need help in several areas. This book is intended to give that help. First, even most committed Catholics need additional understanding of Catholic teaching on marriage. Everyone knows that the Catholic Church is "against divorce," for instance, but most young couples don't exactly know why. Still less do they know how to avoid divorce. Every Catholic who intends to marry knows that the Church considers marriage a special and solemn thing—a sacrament. But in addition to a now dusty memory from your Confirmation class— what is a sacrament? And how does marriage fit the definition?

In short, this book is designed to present in concise form not only the Catholic "rules" about marriage, but also the thinking behind them. This thinking is grounded in Sacred Scripture and the teachings of Christ. It is also grounded in two thousand years of Sacred Tradition, guided by the Holy Spirit and proclaimed by the teaching authority of the Church. Furthermore, it is based on reason and common sense. It follows that Catholic teaching on marriage is true and realistic.

I present this book with the profound conviction that we need more preparation than ever before for marriage. That is because our society has changed. Not long ago, marriage was held in high esteem. Everyone except social misfits held fairly predictable beliefs about marriage. What's more, almost everyone supported it as an institution and respected married people for their commitment. Now, however, everything is different. More and more, marriage is considered a malleable and changeable institution. More and more, the very definition of marriage is undermined by social and moral movements. More and more, marriage is under fire from relativists and subjectivists. Those who marry now need more preparation to cope with the changed situation. In fact, they need an introduction to the entire concept of Matrimony both as a moral study and as a sacramental one. This book is intended to fill that need.

I invite you readers to look with an unblinking eye at the troubled state of Matrimony in Western culture, and to ask yourselves what kind of union you want. I pray that you will not take the run-down condition of marriage in our society as the last word on the subject. I also pray that you will openly receive what Christ proposes through his Church about marriage. Is this not what being Catholic means? Finally, I pray that with the help of our Savior and His blessed Mother you will enter a holy, joyful, and permanent union.

CHAPTER 1

LOOKING AHEAD:
INVITATION TO CATHOLIC MARRIAGE

Much of this first chapter is general statements of Catholic principles. These often come out looking like "rules." But Catholic teaching is not rules. It is, instead, a Spirit-led guide to moral reality. Want to know the truth? The Church is God's guide to it. A list of principles usually seems a bit blunt and shallow. But please don't let that bother you. This chapter is just a way of indicating what's in the rest of the book, which presents the reasons behind the principles.

I hope, however, that as you proceed you will realize that the Church's reasoning behind her teachings is logical and convincing. Growing in the faith is a lifelong process for a committed Catholic. I pray that this category includes you. That growth consists of acquiring a deeper and deeper understanding of the reasoning behind the easily stated, and easily misunderstood, "rules." *A principle to remember: Catholic norms or rules are always the tip of an iceberg. They represent conclusions from two thousand years of conflict, prayer, study, and decision, all guided by the Holy Spirit. They also serve the prime function of moral law, which is to protect something good that God has given us.*

The challenge of marriage. Your decision to marry is one of the most important choices you will ever make. It will determine your permanent state in life, with all of its obligations, privileges, opportunities, joys, and sorrows. Meeting and experiencing these will be part of your Christian vocation. Marriage will even to some extent *define* you as a person. Consequently, the challenge that you face as you prepare for marriage can hardly be overemphasized. Though joyful, marriage is serious. It is probably as serious (and joyful) as anything else you will ever do. It pertains to your very being. Prepare for it accordingly.

The Church has much to say about "states of life." These are:
- single
- married
- single and consecrated

You have expressed a desire to enter the married state. The Church teaches that a state of life and the life in that state become identical. Since marriage is for life, it takes a lifetime for a complete marriage to come into being. A marriage is not just a ceremony. It comprehends the entire lives of a husband and wife until they are separated by death. That means that the real nature of marriage will become clearer to you through your experience of life together than it is now, for marriage must be *lived* to be truly understood. Nevertheless, vital information about marriage, based on the experience of others and the teaching of the Church, can also be *taught*. That is what this book is for. My purpose is to present briefly the real teachings of the Church on marriage and related subjects. I do so in the belief that genuinely understanding and accepting Catholic teaching on marriage is the best way for a couple, with the help of Christ, to build their own sacramental union.

At the same time, you should understand that the contents of this book merely sketch the reality. One can study marriage for a lifetime and not come to the end of the subject. People actually get PhDs in the theology of marriage. The subject is so complicated because marriage is one of God's mysteries. By *mystery* I don't mean something outlandish or unexplained. I mean, rather, a great truth that cannot be fully explored because the human intellect is limited. The great truths of God's creation are called mysteries because the more you explore them, the deeper meanings they yield. So deep, in fact, that they are without end. If you are married for seventy-five years, you will have a profound understanding of marriage. But you will still be in awe of its mystery. You will still be learning.

Marriage is the oldest human social institution. It is represented first in the Bible by the relationship between our original parents, Adam and Eve (Genesis 1.26-5.5). It was instituted by God Himself, who, in the words of the Second Vatican Council, "made the married state the beginning and foundation of human society.[1] The family is *God's* creation. It is not a human invention. What's more, it mysteriously mirrors its origin, the Holy Trinity. It is also a human universal: though marriage customs may differ, all societies in history have recognized and cultivated marriage.

The Scriptures tell us that marriage is also mysteriously like the relation between Christ and His Church. St. Paul compares the attitude of a good husband toward his wife with Christ's love for the Church, which is His Body: "He who loves his wife loves himself. For no man ever hates his own flesh, but nourishes and cherishes it, as Christ does the Church" (Ephesians 5. 28-29). Further on in the same passage St. Paul also indicates another "great mystery" (Ephesians 5. 32) about Matrimony. This is the fact that in marriage a man and a woman become "one flesh"—that is, a single unit, a sort of spiritual individual. This unit is composed of two complementary beings who have voluntarily entered a permanent union of body, mind, and soul. Very significantly, a married man and woman also form a single unit for having children. This procreative unit is a vital meaning of the phrase "one flesh."

Marriage is so important that the Church calls married life a "vocation" and a "sacrament." A vocation is a lifelong calling. Vocations require a great deal of thought and prayer. Obviously, one should not enter into a lifelong calling lightly. You would no more get married suddenly or without preparation than you would become a priest suddenly. To live in a marriage as Jesus teaches us is to engage not in an ordinary human pursuit but in a divinely given "apostolate." To enter the married state is to accept a vocation from God, just as a priest or a religious brother or sister answers God's call. Like those other vocations, marriage requires preparation, discernment, prayer, and obedience to God's laws.

Sadly, marriage is also a battleground. Present critics have called into question the validity of marriage and even its very definition. Some people now consider marriage a mere matter of convenience or pleasure. They think that marriage can be entered without much thought and ended when the fun seems to be over. Divorce prevails in modern Western society. Many people have concluded that stable, permanent marriages are rarely possible now. Some don't even think them desirable. They like the idea of an easily entered, easily dissolved "marriage."

This situation is new. It has not been many decades since everyone agreed on the nature of marriage. A nuptial ceremony or the beginning of a marriage was defined in a dictionary as "a mutual and voluntary" vow of a man and woman, ratified in a public rite, "to live together as husband and wife until separated by death."[2] Now, however, many people are not so sure. Inadequate education, popular entertainment, faulty ethics, and even some religions are largely focused on the individual's *self-realization*. But this emphasis denies the *self-sacrifice and mutual self-giving* that typify Christian married life. This individualistic focus is opposed to genuine commitment to another person of the opposite sex "for better or for worse." Such thorough control does Satan have of our popular culture that some people even think marriage is possible between two men or two women.

Pope John Paul II clearly indicates the situation:

At times it appears that concerted efforts are being made to present as "normal" and attractive, and even to glamorize, situations which are in fact "irregular." Indeed, they contradict "the truth and love" which should inspire and guide relations between men and women, thus causing tensions and divisions in families, with grave consequences particularly for children. The moral conscience becomes darkened; what is true, good and beautiful is deformed; and freedom is replaced by what is actually enslavement.[3]

We can be grateful that in this situation, Catholic teaching offers a firm ground on which to base one's married life. But it is a *challenge*. Real marriages are getting to be the exception—an exception that you and I should strive to make less rare. A loyal Catholic family looks strange to the cynics who deny the permanent reality of marriage. But God calls you to be just such a "sign of contradiction"—a Catholic family, loyal within itself and loyal to the teachings of the Church.

One of the underlying ideas behind this book is that you as a couple have the opportunity to be a beacon of light and truth in a world that is staggering in the dark. This is part of your vocation. The decay of fidelity all around us challenges you to be faithful. The removal of God from civil marriage challenges you to put Him foremost in your marriage. You are called to affirm the divine origin of the family and to commit yourselves unconditionally to a true sacramental union. In a Catholic marriage, God and the Church call you to this kind of union. And to nothing less.

Catholic marriage. The dictionary definition of marriage quoted above is secular. But it still reflects an understanding of marriage

that has been almost universally accepted for most of the Christian era, both in the Church and in society at large. Specifically, it says that *a validly contracted marriage*
• *exists only between a man and a woman and*
• *lasts until the death of one of the spouses.*
This understanding is derived from Scripture and from the teaching of the Catholic Church, which is based on Scripture (see Mark 10.2-9).

No amount of twisted Scriptural misinterpretation can negate the fact that Christ Himself taught the permanence of marriage. Therefore, the first necessary feature of Catholic teaching on marriage is:

• Marriage is permanent. A valid marriage can be ended only by death. The infidelity of one spouse—or of both—does not end it. Still less can it be ended by boredom or "falling out of love."

The Church also teaches that:
• The purpose of marriage is the building of Catholic families. This purpose is fulfilled in two parts: (1) the union between husband and wife, which is a blessing from God; and (2) children, another blessing from God and a result of this union.
• No marriage that deliberately excludes children is valid. Consequently, a married couple must be ready to accept children as a gift from God. This doesn't mean that a naturally sterile couple cannot marry validly. It does mean that their union must be open to children if God should choose to bless them with any.
• Sexual relations belong in marriage only. *The Church teaches that all extramarital sex, including that of engaged couples, is seriously wrong.*
• Every sex act must be open to the transmission of life. This requirement, however, allows for the limitation of family size, when necessary, *by natural family planning, but not by artificial means.* The Church teaches that contraception is always wrong. What's more, contraception has had disastrous effects on the family and society. Its damages are only now being understood, and only by a few.

• Marriage is a *sacrament*, and the married man and woman are in a very real sense its *ministers*. In the family sphere husband and wife are empowered by Christ in their own unique ministry. They make Christ present to each other. An analogy is the way in which a priest makes Christ present in the confessional. I will return to this subject in Chapter 3.

Love. The Church asks you to learn and adopt a concept of love different from that accepted by our society, in which love is usually misunderstood. Our society makes two principal mistakes about love.

• First we often wrongly equate love with sexual relations. Even our language reflects this mistake, as the phrase "making love" demonstrates.

• Second, we are mistaken when we think of love primarily as a feeling. It is much more.

Genuine love is not limited in these ways. Sex is only a part of love and very often has nothing at all to do with it. Wouldn't it be nonsense to speak of "making love" to a prostitute—or to someone you have just met? And yet sex with near or total strangers is the common stuff of popular entertainment now.

Since the "sexual revolution" of the 1960s our culture has increasingly approved of whatever anyone wants to do sexually. But such a license has nothing to do with Christianity, even though many who call themselves Christians endorse it. You who are called to Catholic marriage are called to recover a Scriptural and Catholic understanding of the virtue of *chastity*, without which Christian marital love cannot exist. Though sex is an important and wonderful gift from God, it occupies only a small part of the time and energy a married couple must spend with each other. Sometimes sex must be completely absent. Furthermore, it is a totally inadequate basis for commitment. Consequently, couples who intend marriage should ask themselves honestly if their mutual attraction is chiefly sexual. If your attraction to each other is mainly based on sex, you should carefully reexamine their intention to marry. Note that you can't be objective about this if you are already sharing the same bed.

Feelings are also good in themselves, for they are part of God's creation, which the Lord declared at the beginning to be "very good" (Genesis 1.31). Jesus Himself was subject to the full range of human emotions. But He had control over them. Adults, especially Christians, must not let feelings run their lives. They must follow Christ in this matter. Though He felt and expressed emotions— affection, distress, grief, indignation, dread—Jesus always kept His feelings subordinate to His will to obey the Father. Likewise, our commitment to a Christian life is a matter of intellect. It is *chosen*, not produced by hormones. Our feelings often have to be ignored when right and wrong are involved. Therefore, Christians must use non-emotional guides to right thinking and conduct. We must form our consciences by the teachings of the Church, whose long, Spirit-guided experience has produced an unrivaled treasure of wisdom about the conduct of human life.

• *Genuine Christian marital love includes all forms of what people call love. These include affection, sexual love, friendship, Christian charity, attraction, and sentiment.[4] The essence of real marital love is freely willed self-giving based on the value of one's spouse as a* person.[5]

• *Christian charity must overshadow and govern all the other kinds of love. Like the divine love from which it comes, Christian charity seeks the genuine good of the loved one. This means doing what is right in the sight of God even when one's feelings must be sacrificed. Christian love or charity is more an act of the will than of the emotions.*

• *Sometimes real love actually requires* overcoming *strong feelings in order to do what is right.*

This love is the only sort that merits the name. It is the kind of love that Christ showed to the human race. Its nature in marriage will become clearer as this book proceeds.

The Christian family. In the teaching of the Catholic Church, the family is the most important social unit. Other parts of society—government, schools, businesses, entertainment enterprises, and so forth—are less important than the family. In fact, Catholic social teaching states firmly that all other social structures must serve the interests of the family. Therefore it is wrong for government to pass a law that weakens family structure. It is also wrong for a business to sell or provide a product or service that undermines the rightful authority of parents. Giving contraceptives and providing abortions to teenagers are examples of how evil this wrong can be.

The family is the focus of much Catholic teaching. Obviously, having a Catholic understanding of the family is a necessary part of Catholic marriage preparation. Nevertheless, many details of Catholic teaching on the family are beyond the scope of this book. Chapter 5 includes basic Catholic teaching on children as one of the primary goods and ends of marriage. But such matters as child-raising are not covered. The practical principles of family finance and stewardship in Chapter 8 are also of vital importance to family life in Christ. Nevertheless, their details lie beyond the scope of this book. Couples who read this book should study Catholic teaching on the rearing of children. They should also read some of the works listed in Chapter 10, which are sources both for this book and for further enrichment.

The moral life. Underlying the Catholic teaching on marriage is the Church's moral teaching. Many Catholics need to be reminded that right and wrong are not a matter of opinion. Good and evil belong to the real, objective order of creation. The phrase "objective moral law" means that the law really exists, independent of human opinion. Therefore, to change the moral law is not only beyond the rights of any human culture, but literally beyond its ability. The Church herself cannot change the moral law. The Church, guided by the Holy Spirit, teaches that the Ten Commandments are as much a part of objective reality as any scientific fact. In any culture, for instance, intentionally killing an innocent human being is objectively wrong. This would be true *even if everyone in that society thought otherwise.* To such laws individual Christians are responsible, regardless of public opinion or cultural habit. Moral right and wrong are not determined by majority opinion.

A Catholic whose conscience is shaped by a culture in opposition to the Church's teaching needs to change his way of judging and acting. If, for instance, you have learned to approve of sexual relations outside marriage, I pray that you will reflect on the teaching of Scripture and the Church and strive to conform to it. Better to conform to it than to the "spirit of the age." *"The judgment of conscience does not establish the law.*"[6] This profound truth, as here restated by Pope John Paul II, has great significance for how we as Catholics must live in an increasingly pagan society. We cannot look to society to inform our consciences. We must go to the unchanging revelation of the Father and Creator to find out what is right and wrong. The Church is our guide for doing so.

The Church solemnly teaches, "Human acts are moral acts because they express and determine the goodness or evil of the individual who performs them . . . . [T]hey give moral definition to the very person who performs them, determining his *profound spiritual traits.*"[7] Our acts therefore have real consequences of eternal significance for us and the people we influence. Our thoughts, words, and deeds will determine where we spend eternity. Especially pertinent to this book, individuals preparing for marriage are in a sense *creating* themselves morally.

It is easy enough to see the wrong that is all around us. Look at the consequences of ignoring the teaching of Christ. Divorce among Catholics has soared along with "trial marriages" and contraception. "Value-free" sex education has had exactly the opposite effect of its stated intention. Neutral sex education and contraception were sold as a means of preventing social ills. But instead, they have caused teenage pregnancy, abortion, and sexually transmitted disease to grow like an ugly fungus.

Practically no one—regardless of religious or political affiliation—thinks the moral status quo in our society is acceptable. A sense of moral crisis reigns. It is my hope and prayer that every couple who use this book will strive to see their lives, both before and after marriage, in the mirror of eternity, and to conduct themselves accordingly. It is time for all people, especially Catholics, to acknowledge honestly the harm done by the sexual revolution, and to reject that ill-guided movement and all its parts.

What power God gives us! He lets us make of ourselves what we will, either in conformity with His truth or in opposition to it. The moral self that an individual brings to a marriage consequently has a great deal to do with whether the marriage succeeds. Recently the daughter of a rich man of my acquaintance was married in a large southwestern city. Her father, who is in his fourth "marriage," publicly wished her *good luck*—as if to say that his luck had not been so good. But successful marriage is not a matter of luck. It is a matter of making the right choices, all of which have moral significance, and of *committing* oneself to the marital vocation. God will help you keep a genuine commitment. He calls *you*, a couple preparing for marriage, to be a "sign of contradiction" to the wrongs that have damaged marriage in our society.

God calls us all to transformation in His Son. Your marriage can be a large part of your transformation or can actually prevent it. The choice, which must be made in a thousand situations during the years to come, is yours.

The ceremony. Chapter 9 of this book is about planning your wedding ceremony. Here is my preliminary advice on this matter:

- Prayerfully consider the various readings and other elements that will make up your ceremony. *Consult a priest or deacon. Make sure from the beginning that you are following the guidelines of the Church, the diocese, and the parish in which you are marrying.*
- Remember that the flowers, decorations, music, clothes, invitations, seating, gifts, reception, pictures, and other transitory elements of your wedding *are much less important* than the fact that you are marrying in Christ. Make this the main guide to your preparation. *Don't let superficial considerations overshadow spiritual realities.* The Church calls on you to remember that your marriage vows—your" words of consent—define the common good of the couple and of the family. First, the common good of the spouses: love, fidelity, honor, the permanence of their union until death." And afterward, the "good of the children. The common good, by its very nature, both unites individual persons and ensures the true good of each."[8]

Discussion questions

1. Why is building a real marriage a challenge?
2. After your marriage do you expect to "live happily ever after"? If not, why not.
3. How do you think preparation for marriage will help you to meet the challenge? What elements of marriage are you not prepared for?
4. Why do you want to get married in the Catholic Church?

Notes to Chapter 1

(1) *Decree on the Apostolate of Lay People* (*Apostolicam Actuositatem*), no. 11, in Documents of Vatican II, ed. Austin P. Flannery (Northport, New York: Costello, 1975).

(2) *New Standard Dictionary of the English Language* (New York and London: Funk and Wagnalls, 1913).

(3) Pope John Paul II, *Letter to Families*, no. 5 (Boston: Pauline Books & Media, 1994).

(4) The first four of these types of love come from C. S. Lewis, *The Four Loves* (New York: Harcourt, Brace & World, 1960). I highly recommend this book.

(5) These next aspects of love are based on Karol Wojtyla (Pope John Paul II), *Love and Responsibility* (New York: Farrar, Straus and Giroux, 1981).

(6) Pope John Paul II, *The Splendor of Truth* (Veritatis Splendor), no. 60 (Boston: St. Paul Books & Media, 1993). My emphasis.

(7) Ibid., no. 71. Italics in original.

(8) Pope John Paul II, *Letter to Families*, no. 10.

Journey of Faith:

CHAPTER 2

BEGINNING PREPARATION

Choosing the married state. Catholic teaching speaks of "states of life." Marriage is one of these. The others are single life in the world and single life in the Church as a priest or religious brother or sister. That's all. Throughout the history of the Church a vocation to the priesthood or the religious life has been thought of as a special calling, and rightly so. Nevertheless, in recent years the theology of marriage and the understanding of vocation have developed a great deal. Now we understand better than in the past that *everyone* has a true vocation from God. For most people, marriage is a part of this vocation.

Although priests and religious are set aside for a high and demanding sacrificial life, the Church has clarified how married life itself is considered a special calling. It, too, requires a life of sacrifice. All members of the Church (indeed, all human beings) are especially called by God to embody Christ in their lives. Just how they are to do this, however, differs from state to state.

The chosen state of life determines, for instance, what sexual activity is moral. What is acceptable for a married person is forbidden to a priest. *But chastity is required in all states of life.* Although chastity is often thought of as an exotic requirement that applies only to clergy and religious, the teaching of Christ demands it of everyone. The reason that we think of it as strange is that the word *chastity* is often misused to mean *celibacy*. All human beings, however, are morally obligated to be chaste. All singles are obligated to be celibate. This is what *chastity* means for them. Chaste behavior for married people obviously differs sharply from chaste behavior for singles.

> • *Marriage changes one's life fundamentally and permanently, just as ordination to the priesthood changes a man's life.*

When priests or religious enter permanently upon a vocational commitment, the commitment becomes the central feature of their lives. Likewise, when they marry, a man and woman take on new roles that permanently alter them. Marriage cannot be a sideline activity. The married state will be central to your life. It can't be something added incidentally to an array of life choices already made. It reorients all elements of one's life. The married man and woman are no longer what they were when single, and they are not simply two units permanently tied together. They are a new creature in Christ, "one flesh."

• *This is one reason the Church considers divorce impossible for a validly married couple: a real marriage brings about a permanent change that cannot be reversed by a legal document.*

As the term "state of life" suggests, marriage involves a basic change, a change in a couple's very being. They are in a sense one new creature that did not exist before their wedding. They are a new spiritual being before the Lord. After the wedding, therefore, cultivating a good marriage is a central concern, an essential part of what God demands.

• *Pursuit of this vocation requires just as much daily attention as pursuit of the priestly vocation.*

Marriage—not just a wedding ceremony but a lifelong commitment—cannot be taken for granted. For this reason, a couple who plan to marry should do everything in their power to prepare themselves for fulfilling their calling. Get ready to work at it.

Beginning preparation for marriage comprises two main points: (1) moral readiness to live in accord with God's will and (2) eligibility for marriage.

(1) Moral readiness: cohabitation and marriage preparation. Not long ago a young couple preparing for marriage reported on their Engaged Encounter weekend to the clergyman overseeing their preparation. They stated that of the thirteen couples in the group, all calling themselves Catholic, they were the only ones not already living together. I believe that this report reflects the reality all across America. It also indicates a genuine crisis of morality in what is sometimes called the "American Church." It means that the Church of the future is now being populated by members who consider the solemn moral teaching of Scripture and the Church irrelevant to their lives. It means that all of these nominal Catholics actually reject the teaching authority of the Church on the subject

of sex and marriage. For them, "Catholic" is more what they want to be *called* than how they want to live.

Part, or most, of the blame for this situation lies with priests and deacons who are uncomfortable confronting couples with the truth. Cowardice sometimes poses as a "pastoral approach." But it is not an act of love to suppress the truth in this matter. Whole dioceses have adopted the policy of simply not bringing the subject of sexual sin up in marriage preparation. Many couples who come to the Church for marriage preparation still expect the Church to uphold the moral law. Individually, these couples have a chance to make good marriages if they repent. They should be challenged to do so. That is the purpose of this section.

My experience has shown that most young couples who have fallen into the sinful trap of cohabitation before marriage respond favorably to a clergyman's demand that they separate in order to prepare for their wedding. Indeed, this is what must happen if the preparation is to be real. If, for financial reasons, a couple would find true hardship in separating, they should make a solemn promise to sleep in separate rooms and refrain from sexual intercourse until married. They should also go to *Confession* often so as to receive the grace of the sacrament of Penance in resisting further sin. In addition, they should realize that their actions put the Church in a difficult position. If the Church seems to approve their cohabitation, others could be led into sin. This is the basic meaning of the word *scandal*. In order to minimize scandal, the couple should let their parents and other relatives know about their promise of abstinence.

Just what *is* the Church's teaching on cohabitation? We need to be perfectly clear in order to dispel the reigning confusion.

• Sex outside of marriage is prohibited by the Sixth Commandment: "You shall not commit adultery" (Exodus 20.14).
• Fornication—sexual acts on the part of unmarried people—is emphatically and repeatedly condemned by St. Paul.

In First Corinthians 6.9-10, for instance, St. Paul writes: "Do not be deceived; neither the immoral, nor idolaters . . . nor thieves, nor the greedy, nor drunkards, nor revilers, nor robbers will inherit the kingdom of God." The word translated "the immoral" is the Greek word for "fornicators." *Christianity puts fornicators in the company of thieves and robbers and teaches that none of them "will inherit the kingdom of God."* Therefore the Church has always taught that sexual relations between unmarried people are gravely wrong. That is, for Catholics who have been taught the moral law, fornication is mortally sinful. *We Catholics have no right to ignore the solemn moral teaching of Scripture and the Church under any condition. Mortal sin separates people from God.*

One may say in their favor, however, that couples are often misled into moral blindness about living together. No wonder, when flawed sex-education programs have pushed them toward sexual activity throughout their schooling; when even the government encourages unmarried sex by showering contraceptives on youth; when nearly all new movies show unmarried characters—stars taken as "role models"—copulating as soon as they feel like it. For Hollywood, sexual relations between unmarried people are a mere matter of course. For the glitterati, sex is just a way of getting to know each other or of letting off steam. The social pressure of such widespread endorsement of fornication is tremendous. In its onslaught many Church leaders have retreated from teaching sexual morality. Many young people have been misled.

Strangely, though, sexual relations are not a good way to get to know someone as a person. *Sexual activity actually keeps a young man and woman from knowing each other as they should in order to prepare for marriage.* One young woman who was living with her boyfriend got into financial trouble. When she was asked if they had discussed finances, she said, "We don't know each other well enough to talk about money!" Their absorption in sex had led to an *illusion of intimacy.* Their sexual relations were causing them to ignore the fundamental practicalities of their situation. Cohabitation actually *prevents* preparation for marriage in many ways. In particular, it keeps people from thinking clearly about each other. You simply cannot rationally consider whether you *ought* to marry a particular person when the two of you are already sexually involved.

Living together before marriage has bad practical effects:
•Denial of the moral law doesn't end at the altar.

When it was first popularized among professing Christians, co-habitation was presented as a "trial marriage." This was to be a period during which a young man and woman could get to know each other so that they would know if they wanted to go ahead with marriage. But what they *really* learn is that sex outside of marriage is okay. Nothing could be more potentially fatal to a marriage. Why? When a young man and woman who are already living together present themselves for marriage preparation, *both of them have already accepted the idea that adultery is no big deal.* Once they have accepted this fallacy, however, what is to keep them from retaining it after marriage? The ceremony? But they have already denied the necessity of the ceremony. They have already rejected the idea that a public, religious marital commitment is necessary to legitimate what they are doing. *In short, they have already told themselves that going outside of marriage for sexual adventures is morally acceptable.* The practical effects can be witnessed in any divorce court.

- *By definition, this relationship is not a commitment. It is tentative and provisional, as commitments are not. The phrase "tentative commitment" is an oxymoron, as is the phrase "trial marriage."*

I (and probably you) have heard many times, from people who end up changing sexual partners over and over, "We are really committed to each other." Isn't that silly? If they were really committed, there would be no question of deciding if they want to marry.

- *If marriage is a sacrament, "trial marriage" is a sacrilege.*

I will return to the sacramentality of marriage in Chapter 3. Meanwhile, think about this parallel: what if a candidate to the priesthood entered a "trial priesthood" and celebrated invalid Masses, gave invalid absolution for sin, and otherwise pretended to represent Christ in the sacraments? We would say that he was committing sacrilege. A married Christian man and woman are ministers of Christ in the sacrament of marriage. Unmarried people have no more right to the privileges of marriage than a layman has to celebrate Mass.

- *Cohabitation leads to increased divorce.*

Divorce is an increasingly serious problem in our society and in the Church. It is often considered a desirable solution for marital problems. Sometimes it may be necessary for self-preservation. But those occasions are rare. The teaching of Jesus on divorce is quite clear:

> Pharisees came up and in order to test Him asked, "Is it lawful for a man to divorce his wife?" He answered them, "What did Moses command you?" They said, "Moses allowed a man to write a certificate of divorce, and to put her away." But Jesus said to them, "For your hardness of heart He wrote you this commandment. But from the beginning of creation, 'God made them male and female.' 'For this reason a man shall leave his father and mother and be joined to his wife, and the two shall become one.' So they are no longer two but one. What therefore God has joined together, let not man put asunder" (Mark 10.2-9).

Clearly, the Son of God teaches that marriage was instituted by the Creator and that a mere human decision embodied in a "certificate of divorce" has no validity.

Following the lead of her Master, the Church teaches that divorce is impossible for a validly married couple. Nevertheless, *partly as a result of cohabitation*, the divorce rate among Catholics has kept up with that of society at large. Far from enhancing marriage, "trial marriage" has produced domestic disaster. In fact, the rate of marital failure among those who live together before marriage is *far higher* than among those who don't: *seventy percent* of those who live together in "trial marriages" fail at the real thing!

This should be a very sobering message to cohabiting couples who come to marriage preparation. They have made their job more difficult by their actions. They will have to try harder than chaste couples. Nevertheless, a sincere effort at remedying the damage can remove the difficulty. *This includes separation until marriage, a deliberate change of heart, much prayer, and resort to the sacrament of Penance (Reconciliation).* One thing to remember: When God forgives sins, we are completely renewed in Christ. Chastity can be recovered through the sacrament of Penance. God will bless the marriages of those who repent and really strive to do His will.

• *Contraception is a further cause of great harm in cohabitation.*

Another plague that has inflated the divorce rate is contraception. This immoral practice is usually automatically accepted as one of the conditions of cohabitation. But its effect on marriage is bad, and it compounds the evil of fornication. It is used, after all, to avoid the consequences of breaking the Sixth Commandment. The historical relation between contraception and divorce is clear: contraception has grossly enlarged the percentage of divorces. *But the divorce rate among those who adhere to the Church's moral teaching about contraception has not risen.* I will have more to say on this subject, and the related subject of natural family planning, in Chapter 5. Here, however, the point is that if a couple are cohabiting, they are generally also violating the moral law by using artificial means to avoid pregnancy. Furthermore, they are living in a state of sin, according to the Scriptures and the solemn teachings of the Church. They are using one moral wrong to prevent the consequences of another. We should not think we escape the moral consequences of this false remedy.

Contraception is like sterilization. I once heard a remark made to a man who had just had a vasectomy: "You will probably become the neighborhood stud now." That, I suggest, is the underlying type of false freedom conferred by contraception. It distorts the truth in many ways:

• It promotes the idea that sexual pleasure should be pursued without care or obligation.
• It says that children are a curse rather than God's greatest blessing.
• It reduces the dignity of its users by technologically altering them like animals.

The intimacy that accompanies contraception is therefore not true intimacy. Contraceptive sex is *use* of another person as an object for self-satisfaction. If real love is the true vocation of human persons,[1] contraceptive sex is antihuman. What kind of genuine love is it that says, "I love you, but only if you are temporarily sterile?"

Sex before marriage is not marital love but a dangerous sideline. A great Christian philosopher, Joseph Pieper, writes:

On the one hand, the sexual act can take place without love and even without love in the narrower erotic sense. On the other hand, love between man and woman, understood as the closest imaginable union of *persons*, includes in addition to sexuality many quite other things—so much so that a sexuality set apart and therefore "absolutized" tends rather to block love, even erotic love, and to alienate people from one another as personal beings.[2]

(2) Impediments to marriage. Your priest or deacon advisor will ask you a series of questions to determine your eligibility to marry. Most or all dioceses in the United States have questionnaires designed for the purpose. The preliminary questionnaire can help determine what to do next.

Certain factors can render couples ineligible for marriage. These are known as impediments to marriage. They are based on the nature of the sacrament of Matrimony and on the experience of the Church. Some of the legalities involved in impediments are complicated, since they come from 2,000 years of observation. Most couples need not be concerned with the technicalities, however, if they meet a few necessary conditions:

• If either of them has been legally married before, the couple may not marry until the Church has declared the married party free to do so.

This means that the married party must apply for an annulment. The question of annulment is very important in our climate of easy divorce, and it cannot be treated here in any detail. You should understand, however, that the purpose of the procedure is to *protect* the institution of marriage.

If you are already involved in a legal marriage and want to marry in the Catholic Church, you should approach the Church as your helper and friend, not your adversary. A priest or deacon will help with the forms and answer your questions. You should know that the decision, however, does not rest with an individual priest or deacon but with a Church court called the marriage tribunal. If you need to apply for an annulment, you should do so with faith, hope, and charity, knowing that God is all good and that all He does is good. The Church wants to help those who should marry to do so; she wills the true happiness of all. Nevertheless, *the proper atti-*

tude of the petitioner in an annulment suit is one of submission and obedience. You should be resolved to obey the will of God even if it is not what you wish.

As our understanding of the human mind has developed, we have come to understand better how often consent is defective for one reason or another. This means that the tribunal frequently finds that the attempted marriage was in fact not a true marriage. It also means that preparation for marriage should be more thorough to prevent further null marriages. That is one of the purposes of this book.

• If you are a close blood relative of your fiance(e), you cannot marry.

• If you are an ordained priest or deacon, or if you are a consecrated member of a religious order pledged to celibacy or virginity, you cannot marry.

• If you are unable to consummate a marriage sexually, you cannot marry. An impotent man, or a woman psychologically incapable of copulation, cannot marry.

• A boy younger than sixteen or a girl younger than fourteen cannot marry. These ages are specified in canon law, the law of the Church; they can be (and are) raised by the bishops of various countries.

 » *The following are* not *impediments to marriage*:
• Difference of religion.

The Church now blesses many mixed marriages. These are mostly between Catholics and people of other Christian faiths, but sometimes between Catholics and the nonbaptized. Those between Catholics and other Christians are far more numerous.

It has always been the hope of the Catholic Church that Protestants and other non-Catholic Christians would come to share the fullness of faith with the Mother Church of Christendom. Toward this end the Church, steadfastly led by the Holy Father, prays constantly for unity among Christians. But she also recognizes the saving power of Christ already at work in faiths that are separated from her. The documents of the Second Vatican Council make this fact clear.

If you are a member of a non-Catholic Christian communion, you will be welcome to marry a son or daughter of the Church. The priest or deacon who prepares you for marriage will help you to receive permission. You cannot marry in the Church until you receive it. Your goal during marriage preparation is to become familiar with the Church's teaching, to which your future spouse *must* adhere and *in which your children must be raised. Your solemn, signed agreement to this condition is required before you can marry in the Church.* Practically speaking, your understanding of the Catholic faith is very important. After all, Catholicism has formed the soul of your future spouse, which you want to know intimately. For this reason I urge you to study the faith deliberately, whether by reading on your own or attending classes at church or studying in some other way. Ask your priest or deacon for suggestions. My belief is that attending classes and studying Catholic teaching together will greatly benefit *both* partners in the marriage.

• Current pregnancy (or parenthood). Of course this is no bar to marriage. But notice these points:

••Pregnancy does not automatically mean that the couple *should* marry.

If they are not suited to a lifelong Christian commitment to each other, marriage will be a mistake. If their mutual attraction is mostly sexual, marriage will not help them. What's more, it will probably bring their child into a strife-torn, doomed marriage. One big mistake is enough.

An unmarried pregnant woman is sometimes better off bearing the child and giving it up for adoption than marrying just because she is pregnant. This is also often better for her child. With the help of God, especially through the Sacrament of Penance, she can regain control of her life and pursue her vocation in a Godly way. A single mother who has been treated like a mere sex object will do better to wait until she finds a man who will love her as a person in Christ. Marrying that man will be preferable to marrying her child's irresponsible father.

•• Pregnancy or parenthood does *not* mean that the couple should continue to live together before marriage.

Again, one mistake must not be used as an excuse for another. Instead, the couple should separate and prepare mentally and spiritually for the sacrament of Matrimony just like any other couple.

Sexual relations will prevent their preparation even if they are already parents. Through the miraculous bounty of God, their premature sexual intimacy has been greatly blessed. God blesses us and offers us opportunities for redemption even when we sin. In order to grasp these opportunities, if they continue with their intention to marry, the pregnant woman and her child's father need to work to prepare for Christian parenthood at the same time that they prepare for marriage. This is, of course, a double task, and doubly hard. But if the shoe fits, wear it. *Don't take this matter for granted.* Like marriage, raising children in modern American society requires all of the planning, effort, and prayer you can come up with. Success will not come automatically.

Discussion questions

1. How can cohabitation lead to increased divorce?
2. How has divorce adversely affected you or someone you know?
3. What is the connection between promiscuity and divorce?
4. Why doesn't adultery justify a divorce?
5. What effects can one's attitude toward divorce have on the validity of a marriage?
6. Why is a "trial marriage" not a real commitment?

Notes to Chapter 2

(1) Cf. Karol Wojtyla (Pope John Paul II), *Love and Responsibility* (New York: Farrar, Straus and Giroux, 1981), pp. 28-31 and Chapter II.

(2) Josef Pieper, "On Love," in *Faith-Hope-Love* (Ignatius Press, 1997), pp. 247-8. Italics added.

Journey of Faith:

CHAPTER 3

MARRIAGE AS A SACRAMENT AND VOCATION

The sacrament of Holy Matrimony. I have mentioned that Christian marriage is a sacrament of which the marriage partners are *ministers*. The Catholic Church teaches that marriage is one of the seven sacraments. A sacrament is:
> • *a sacred action originated by Christ, blessed by Him, or both, and*
> • *instituted by Him in His Church as a sign*
> • *by which He comes in the person of a minister to His people, gives them grace, forms them into His body, and prepares them for eternal life in His kingdom.*

Catholics are generally accustomed to thinking of the Eucharist as fitting this definition more than the other sacraments. Faithful Catholics often witness the Sacrifice of the Mass and hear how the consecrated elements actually become the Body and Blood of Christ. We know that the priest at Mass is acting as Jesus did at the Last Supper, and that Christ comes to us bodily in Holy Communion. Thoughtful and obedient Catholics also know that celebrating the Eucharist is a lifelong, solemn, weekly obligation. The Sacrifice of the Mass is therefore an ongoing means of constituting ourselves as the Body of Christ, of forming ourselves in His image. That is what this sacrament does.

When it comes to marriage, however, our thinking may falter. We often think of the *sacrament* as being the ceremony itself—a one-time affair. Marriage, we seem to believe, happens when we stand up nervously before our relatives and say "I do." Subsequent married life is thought of as something else, though we don't quite know what.

The real relationship of the *sacrament* to the whole of married life is not much talked about. This is one reason most married people are unaware of how theirs is a ministerial role. The clergyman at the wedding is a minister, true. He represents Christ and the Christian community in conveying a sacramental blessing to the union of the couple. The clergyman is necessary for the sacramentality of their marriage. He blesses their union as Christ blessed the marriage at Cana (John 2). *But, by the work of God, the marrying couple themselves are the ones who bring the union about. They do so through their solemn consent, or vows.*

After the ceremony, people often think of the sacramental feature of marriage as being somehow located in the past, on their wedding day. But this is not an adequate understanding of marriage. *It is the entire marriage, "until death do us part," that constitutes the sacrament of Matrimony.* God has chosen to be present in the details of our daily lives. This is especially true of the relationship between man and woman in the sacrament of marriage.

All too often couples say to themselves, in effect, "The sacrament is over. Now to get down to routine." But the sacrament is not something that occurs and then fades, remaining only a nice but shrinking memory. *The sacrament is Christ made present daily throughout married life, through His ministers, the married man and woman. Their life together is a sign of His presence.*

It follows that the ministry involved in the sacrament also continues throughout the lives of the married couple. Each day every validly married man is called upon both to represent Christ to his wife and to see Christ in her. She is similarly obligated to him. They are able to fulfill their sacramental roles because they are changed by their union with each other into ministers of Christ. This change cannot be undone, although one may fail to live up to it, just as a priest can be inactive in his ministry.

We are called to image Christ to everyone we meet. That is our general social obligation as Christians. Married people image Christ to each other also, but in a special way. Theirs is a lifelong vocation to a commitment to each other. It is more demanding than our general obligation to live in Christian charity, not less. This is true specifically because of the sacramental nature of marriage.

How does marital love resemble other forms of Christian charity?

• First, the surface resemblance is clear. Jesus teaches that the Works of Mercy are necessary: "Truly, I say to you, as you did it to one of the least of these my brethren, you did it to me" (Matthew 25.40). The Golden Rule—"Do unto others as you would have them do unto you" (Matthew 7.12)—

applies to our dealings with *all* other human beings, including our spouses.

• The obligation to charity in marriage is primary. If "charity begins at home," as we often hear, one is *more* obliged to see Christ in his wife than in a needy stranger. The general obligation both to see Christ in others and to image Him in ourselves is deepened and intensified in marriage.

• But marital charity is also different *in kind*. It is a separate case, involving a special sacramental relationship between a man and a woman. Although I should wear the face of Christ in helping the poor, for instance, in doing so I do not act as a minister of one of the Church's special sacraments. I am merely doing my general Christian duty. But married people *do* act as such ministers to each other, and in doing so they assume special obligations.

Jesus has promised to act in a special way through the person of His sacramental ministers. To imitate the Lord in general charity is one thing. To act sacramentally *in persona Christi* is another, though it certainly includes charity. That is why a priest at Mass is no longer just a priest but an effective representative of Christ Himself. Likewise, a partner in a Christian marriage is no longer just a man or woman but the bearer of Christ Himself. *Your* habitual acts of kindness and concern for your spouse will, under God, make Jesus present throughout your life. *If a man and a woman recognize this fact and keep it foremost in their married life, their marriage will not fail.* Not to say that it is always easy. Sometimes you may not act like Christ, but those times will be occasions for you to work especially hard at embodying His image. The sacrament of Penance will help.

Husband and wife as Christ and the Church. The mystery of Christ's presence in a marriage is comparable to that of His presence in the Church. That mysterious analogy helps to explain the sacramental nature of marriage. In Chapter 1, I have mentioned St. Paul's teaching on this subject. St. Paul aligns the Lord with the Bridegroom and the Church with the Bride. Just as Jesus abides with and loves the Church, the groom abides with and loves the wife.

But St. Paul didn't invent that teaching from nothing. The analogy is a New Testament development of a much older theme—the theme of God as a loving Father "married" to His people. The Old Testament speaks of God's creative power and the fecundity or fruitfulness of His people. In this image, the people as a whole is considered feminine, capable of bringing forth children. In Isaiah, for instance, the prophet speaks of the coming "vindication of Jerusalem," when God's people will be given a new name:

> You shall no more be termed Forsaken,
> and your land shall no more be termed Desolate;
> but you shall be called My delight is in her,
> and your land Married;
> for the lord delights in you
> and your land shall be married . . . .
> As the bridegroom rejoices over the bride,
> so shall your God rejoice over you (Isaiah 62.2, 4-5).

And in the book of Revelation, the final book of the New Testament, the image occurs again. The heavenly city—equivalent to the Church Triumphant—is described as the "new Jerusalem . . . prepared as a bride adorned for her husband." The Church is then identified as "the Bride, the wife of the Lamb" (Rev. 21.2, 9).

I don't think that anyone *fully* understands this analogy of husband + wife = Christ + the Church. St. Paul, after all, called it a "great mystery" (Ephesians 5.32). But we don't fully understand the Mass, either. We accept Christ's teaching on it because He rose from the dead and in other ways showed that He is the Son of God. "My thoughts are not your thoughts," God states, "neither are your ways my ways . . . . as the heavens are higher than the earth, so are my ways higher than your ways, and my thoughts than your thoughts" (Isaiah 55.9). Hence the mystery associated with every aspect of the Divine Nature. We don't have to understand God's word fully to accept and appreciate it.

Nevertheless, some important observations are possible about the mystery of marriage as it relates to the Church. St. Paul says that a husband should love his wife "as Christ loves the Church" (Ephesians 5.29). But *how* does the Lord do that? By giving Himself completely to her. The Lord, the Bridegroom, "came not to be served but to serve, and to give His life as a ransom for many"

(Matthew 20.28). Christ's relation to the Church is therefore most importantly a giving, self-sacrificial relationship. This is how a husband should love his wife: by giving his life to her.

I will have something to say about control and authority in marriage—matters that are grossly overemphasized in our culture, which seems obsessed with "power"—in Chapter 7. Here it is enough to note that both partners in a marriage represent Christ sacramentally, and that the relationship of *mutual* love and service is the way they carry out their ministry. Although St. Paul teaches that the husband is the "head of the wife" (Ephesians 5.23), the role of "boss" is not a sacramental role like the role of "wife" and "husband." More on these roles in Chapter 6. Jesus is not the "boss" of the Church, but the Head of the Church. And he expressed this relationship by giving himself totally to her, even to dying for her. It's not a "power" thing.

The vocation to conjugal charity. A more advanced concept of charity is involved. The Holy Father, Pope John Paul II, teaches:

> God is love and in Himself He lives a mystery of personal loving communion. Creating the human race in His own image and continually keeping it in being, God inscribed in the humanity of man and woman the vocation, and thus the capacity and responsibility, of love and communion. Love is therefore the fundamental and innate vocation of every human being.[1]

When you answer God's call to enter the state of Holy Matrimony, you are choosing a particular way in which to fulfill this universal human vocation.

You have probably come to realize by now that a person's vocation is never a simple thing. Although to some extent God lets us decide freely what we will do with our lives, our decisions carry duties with them. Fulfilling these duties is part of our vocation. In addition, all human beings have the general vocation to seek to know and do God's will. Moreover, some aspects of vocation are specified by our birth into particular families and nations: the vocation of son or daughter, father or mother, or citizen. Another aspect of vocation is that all human beings are obligated to utilize their talents for God and the common good. When an ability—to write, read, sing, keep account books, or whatnot—remains unused, part of a vocation is unfulfilled.

Marriage is a deliberately chosen, complex vocation that affects the entire spectrum of one's duties in life. Men and women who marry are called *(vocati)* to *raise* their married life, with the help of Christ, above the level of an ordinary union by the vigorous pursuit of "specifically Christian values"[2] in their relationship. These values are summed up by the Holy Father as "conjugal charity."[3]

Charity means love; it encompasses all real love and reflects the internal love of the Blessed Trinity—the love of the Father toward the Son, and the Holy Spirit who proceeds from them. We partake of divine charity when we strive to let Christ run our lives. Participation in God's charity is based on the understanding that man is a creature of God, who belongs to his Creator first, then to his spouse and family, then to others.

» *Some of the features of conjugal charity are:*

• It involves praying together.
• It mandates a genuinely loving attitude when disputes arise, and not a self-pitying or angry one (see Chapter 7).
• It requires a desire to receive all the blessings of marriage. For that reason it is always open to the gift of children. Children should never be reluctantly or regretfully received, even if they are unplanned.
• It therefore avoids contraception. Conjugal charity involves a self-giving so complete, a mutual understanding so thorough, that there is no room in it for the desire that one's spouse be changed chemically or surgically. "Family planning," in other words, must be done in cooperation with God and nature, not in opposition to them (see Chapter 5).
• If you are not ready for a total commitment to conjugal charity, you are not ready to marry. If you have doubts, *wait.* A commitment to conjugal charity, though easy enough to talk about, is a *commitment to the entirety of the marital vocation as it develops organically from your vows—no matter what happens, "for better or for worse."*

Such is the high calling of marriage. Like other vocations, it is a lifetime affair. Its demands require constant attention and discernment, continual renewal, persistent submission to God's will, and a permanent commitment to solemn promises made in the Church. Marriage is like a building to which one adds bricks daily throughout life.

» *The vocation of "building a Christian family" includes two basic goods—the gift of children and the union between man and woman.*

• The Church teaches that the life of mutual love and support between husband and wife is a fundamental human good that should be cultivated and cherished. The *union* itself is good. Pursuing a more perfect union throughout one's married life is part of the married vocation.

• When children come, raising them in Christ is also part of the marital vocation.

Like all vocations, married life isn't easy. But those who choose the married vocation still constitute the vast majority of human beings. So many people can hardly be wrong. Their testimony is proof that marriage and its rewards are an innate and universal human good. Those who succeed in cultivating genuine marriages and who live in Christ under the gentle yoke of conjugal charity find great joy.

The fact that marriage is universally cultivated does not mean that all marriages are alike or that the marital vocation is some kind of cookie-cutter. Every individual and every couple have an absolutely unique vocation given by God. No two couples and no two individuals are alike in their abilities, interests, and social milieu. This means that every married man and woman have unique opportunities for bearing Christ to each other and for bringing God's grace to the world around them.

The Holy Family as a model of conjugal charity. The Blessed Virgin Mary was the special means of the Incarnation of Christ— the special Person out of all the human race with this particular vocation. According to Catholic teaching, she was chosen and prepared in the eternal mind of God to bear His Son into the world. God might have used other means of saving mankind, but He didn't. He chose to save us by Christ, but not without Mary's cooperation. For her part, she perfectly fulfilled the vocation to which all human beings are called—that of seeking to know God's will and to say Yes to it. In her case, the divine will was directed toward God's becoming man and dwelling among us. At the very beginning, Mary's unhesitating Yes was directed toward her miraculous pregnancy.

So was Joseph's. Joseph, though less important than Mary, is also an instrument of the Incarnation. Both before and after Jesus' birth, Joseph protects Mary and her Son. St. Joseph is the "guardian of Virgins," as a fine old prayer says. When he learns of Mary's unexplained pregnancy, he first intends to end his marriage quietly (according to custom she was already his wife by virtue of their engagement). But, as Pope John Paul says, "The angel of the Lord tells him that this would not be consistent with his vocation; indeed it would be contrary to the spousal love uniting him to Mary."[4]

Note that this vocation is what Joseph has chosen. The love and trust that, even before the formal wedding, binds him to Mary, leads him to accept God's word. He consequently must seek to fulfill his chosen vocation, to which the angel of the Lord recalls him. And that is to love and protect Mary and her Child. Being a "just man," he responds in perfect conjugal charity. As a result, we think of St. Joseph as a breadwinner and family head, honored by Jesus and Mary, who nevertheless let *them* shape the course of his life.

It wasn't easy. Joseph took his young bride to Bethlehem with him. He moved to Egypt to save the Child, and so left his home and business and defied King Herod. When it was safe, he took his family to Nazareth, where Jesus grew up. There Joseph the carpenter died, after a life wholly devoted to his family. That's all we know about him. But that's enough. Throughout the history of the Church, faithful Christians have looked to Joseph as a model father and worker who died a holy death in the bosom of his family.

The scenes from the early life of Christ illustrate the firm foundation on which the Holy Family is built. Mary is at prayer when the angel Gabriel announces the Lord's coming. With obedient love for the law of God, Mary and Joseph present the Child to His Father in the temple. Jesus causes Mary and Joseph anxiety by remaining behind in Jerusalem at the age of twelve. But He still remains obedient to them, even though His own mission to do his "Father's business" draws him toward His death. The Holy Family lives according to the revealed law of God. They treat that law with reverent obedience, not grudging compliance or resentment.

Even after He is grown, Jesus treats His Mother with the greatest deference. At the wedding in Cana, when He works His first miracle, He actually does so in obedience to Mary. Mary, on her side, tells the wine stewards, "Do whatever He tells you" (John 2.5). Isn't this relationship between the grown-up Son and His Mother like the mutual submission that St. Paul says should exist between husband and wife? And isn't it a clear testimony to Christ's overwhelming love for His Mother that He lets her tell Him when to begin His public ministry?

All in all, though only briefly sketched in Scripture, the Holy Family provides us with the supreme model of what a family should be—mutually loving, forbearing, and self-sacrificing. As the Holy Father writes,

> Through God's mysterious design, it was in that family that the Son of God spent long years of a hidden life. It is therefore the prototype and example for all Christian families. It was unique in the world. Its life was passed in anonymity and silence in a little town in Palestine. It underwent trials of poverty, persecution and exile. It glorified God in an incomparably exalted and pure way. And it will not fail to help Christian families—indeed, all the families in the world—to be faithful to their day-to-day duties, to bear the cares and tribulations of life, to be open and generous to the needs of others, and to fulfill with joy the plan of God in their regard.[5]

> Let us all look to Jesus, Mary, and Joseph for their example and help.

Discussion questions

1. What does the word sacrament mean?
2. How is marriage a sacrament?
3. If a vocation is a calling from God, how is marriage a vocation? What part does human choice have in determining one's vocation?
4. Baptism and marriage are both sacraments. If water is the sign of baptism, what is the sign of marriage? Are there any similarities between these two sacraments?

Notes to Chapter 3

(1) Pope John Paul II, *Familiaris Consortio*, no. 11, in *Vatican Council II: More Postconciliar Documents,* ed. Austin Flannery (Grand Rapids, Michigan: Eerdmans, 1982); italics added.

(2) Ibid., no. 13.

(3) Ibid.

(4) Pope John Paul II, *Letter to Families,* no. 20 (Boston: Pauline Books & Media, 1994).

(5) Pope John Paul II, *Familiaris Consortio*, no. 86.

CHAPTER 4

SEXUALITY

Male, female, and human nature. Everyone talks about it. Everyone knows about it. Some preachers rant about it and predict the end of civilization. Sensualists accept it with a smile while scrambling to make it "safe." But no matter what your angle, the truth seems obvious: no society in human history has ever been quite so absorbed in sex as this one. Even mainstream, "family" publications like *Reader's Digest* now feature articles on such subjects as how to find someone to fornicate with or how to have more orgasms. We as a culture seem to think that this is the most important possible subject. We have, in effect, turned into a mindless, leering society. We seem to spend as much time as possible drooling about sexual adventures of every conceivable kind. We call this being "adult."

But there is also a paradox here. Something doesn't fit. At the same time that we have made an idol of sex, we have made it a matter of such routine that talk about it is often more boring than exciting. The pornographic how-to book called *The Joy of Sex* was actually ridiculed some years ago by another title, *The Job of Sex.* As if sex were a bit of predictable daily *work* that one simply had to get through, like going to the office on Monday or taking out the trash. Ho hum. Boring.

This is certainly not what the authors of the sexual revolution wanted. Nor is it what God wants.

The Church was right all along. The fact is that if you take sex away from the sanctity of marriage and start to treat it as the be-all and end-all of human existence, it loses most of its meaning. Strangely, it becomes *less* important. To routinize sex is to make it into no big deal. And that is what we have done by cultivating an obsession with it.

Sexual activity has been downgraded from a sacred union of husband and wife to an ordinary necessity for all, married or unmarried, sexually normal or homosexual. The lesson has not been lost on our children. For many of them, by the time they are midway through adolescence, sex is a matter of course. Everybody does it. It is something you do compulsively but routinely, and it has no special meaning except that it feels good.

The chances are that many readers of this book have been susceptible to this kind of thinking. Make no mistake: *this wrong thinking has been very destructive of the family and family life.* If you have accepted the principles of the sexual revolution, please examine your way of thinking in the light of Church teaching. I would be unfair to you, and would fail in the obligation to charity toward you, if I didn't warn you. *If you have had early and frequent sexual experiences, you are very much in danger of failing in marriage. You have stacked the deck against yourself. Succeeding will require your utmost effort.*

If you have bought into the ethics of the sexual revolution, straightening out your understanding of the real significance of sex in God's scheme of creation must be a priority for you. Otherwise, you will enter marriage without the necessary moral understanding to make a success of it. What it amounts to is this: if you have turned away from Christ and the moral law, you must now turn back with all your heart. Otherwise, your marriage is most likely to fail. I don't want you to fail. Your success is what this book is about. I guarantee you my prayers.

» *Our culture's sexual idolatry has had some odd results:*

• One of these is a *split between sexuality and identity.*

Although a popular feminist book shouts in its title that "our bodies" are the equivalent of "ourselves," in fact modern people divide the two. Even the authors of *Our Bodies Our Selves* divide the two. They try to maintain a split between the body and their essence as people. No matter what they do with their bodies, they think that their "selves" are untouched. Thus it is thought, for instance, that one can be a prostitute and also a very good woman (or boy). Pornographers and pedophiles argue for their own moral normality. One can do almost anything and still consider himself "nice."

More to the point here, it is thought that one can engage in all kinds of sexual experiences and simply turn them off at the altar, remain faithful, and live happily ever after. As if fornication didn't involve the *self* but some *addition* to it, like shoes or clothes. We somehow think that we can put our sexual experiences into a separate compartment from our real selves and simply ditch them when we marry.

But that idea is false. God has given us the profound freedom of constructing ourselves morally by our actions. Your own real, deep moral *self* is determined by your choices. He who chooses to take addictive drugs, for instance, does not remain a mere nice guy who shoots up. He *becomes* an addict, and his entire being is changed. The "doctor" who performs abortions for a living is no longer a doctor, a healer, no matter how much of a good citizen he considers himself. A person who habitually tells lies becomes a liar. Immoral sexual choices come from inside ourselves and alter our souls. The self and what we choose to do are the same thing.

• Another odd result of our society's sexual saturation is the *rejection of true human sexuality.*

The type of feminism that has accompanied the sexual revolution has led to the denial of real differences between men and women. For radical feminists, the biology of the human body is simply an inconvenient and superficial detail. Just beneath the skin, they believe, women are just like men. Male and female differences are just a cultural invention. This idea, like the trivialization of the sex act, has resulted from accepting the false notion that sex does not pertain to the essence of the person but to the surface.

The Scriptures and the Church have always taught otherwise. That does not mean, however, that the Church is opposed to women's progress. But the Church and all right-thinking people are certainly opposed to *false* progress, to destruction posing as reform. From her beginning the Church has proclaimed the high dignity of every human being, male or female. To this extent, the Church has been in the vanguard of institutions devoted to social justice. She has supported such goals as freedom from abuse, equal pay for equal work, and equal opportunity in the marketplace. The equal moral status of men and women before God was taught by Christ, by St. Paul, and by the Church through the ages. All too often these teachings have been ignored or denied by self-centered, power-hungry men with agendas of their own, and that sorry spectacle has given weapons to the radicals. How much better the world would be if all who *profess* Christianity had actually always *listened* to the Church and *obeyed* her.

But that doesn't mean that sexuality can be either trivialized, as in popular culture today, or ignored, as in feminist claims. Clearly, the Church teaches that acceptance of the fundamental importance of sexuality is necessary to the development of people as human beings. A "whole person" is a person whose entire being is an expression of either maleness or femaleness.

> In the context of a culture which seriously distorts or entirely misinterprets the true meaning of human sexuality, because it separates it from its essential reference to the person, the Church more urgently feels how irreplaceable is her mission of presenting sexuality as a value and task of the *whole person*, created male and female in the image of God.[1]

I added the italics to this quotation from the Holy Father, who clearly teaches that sexuality is a fundamental aspect of human beings as *persons*—that is, as creatures made in the image of God, from Whom all *personhood* comes.

According to the Church, sexuality is biological, yes, but it is more. Sexuality "concerns the innermost being of the human person as such."[2] It is not something that can be treated as a superficial element of life, to be altered, for instance, by contraceptives. It is not something that can rightly be used as a plaything with multiple partners in casual relationships. It is, rather, a fundamental part of our identity as human beings. It demands respect and not chemical alteration or casual abuse. For only when sexuality is treated as both a profound truth about human nature and as a sacred aspect of human beings who desire to give themselves totally to each other in marriage can one speak of a Christian or especially a Catholic marital union.

The Church even teaches that human sexuality, which is a basic fact of anthropology, is mysteriously derived from the nature of God Himself. Pope John Paul writes that "The universe, immense and diverse as it is, the world of all living beings, *is inscribed in God's fatherhood, which is its source.*"[3] There is something in the internal nature of the Holy Trinity—something about the interrelation of the Divine Persons—that gives rise to the very idea of interpersonal communion in human society, and particularly in the basic society known as the family. The "pattern and inspiration" of creation is found "in the mystery of His Being, which is already here disclosed as the divine 'We.'" That is why the creation of man in the image of God involves not only the creation of a rational soul but of a species made up of complementary beings known as male and female. From the mystery of the divine We "the human being comes forth by an act of creation: *God created man in His own image,* in the image of God He created him; male and female He created them' (Genesis 1:27)."[4] Is this creation in the image of God not the ultimate basis of the sacramentality of marriage?

Jesus and Genesis. The teaching of Christ about marriage depends directly on this fundamental understanding of human nature. The most important passage in the Bible on the relation of sexuality to the human essence is in the book of Genesis. This is the passage that Jesus refers to when He presents His *own* teaching. Genesis says, "God created man in His own image, in the image of God He created him; male and female He created them" (Genesis 1.27). In these few words the Bible definitively teaches that sexuality is at the very unchangeable core of creation. No one can change this core. No one can opt out of being male or female. A male who has undergone a "sex change" operation, for instance, isn't a female but a mutilated male.

Christ's thinking about this part of Genesis is clear. It underlies His rejection of divorce. I quote this time from Matthew:

> Pharisees came up to Him and tested Him by asking, "Is it lawful to divorce one's wife for any cause?" He answered, "Have you not read that He Who made them from the beginning made them male and female, and said, 'For this reason a man shall leave his father and mother and be joined to his wife, and the two shall become one'? What therefore God has joined together, let no man put asunder" (Matthew 19. 3-6).

In this passage Jesus teaches that the inescapably sexual nature of human beings is the basis for monogamy. *Because* man was created "male and female," He says, a man and a woman leave their parents and "become one." Man and woman are of complementary sexual natures—*"for this reason"* they marry and become one.

Radical feminists reject the idea of complementarity because it suggests that women *need* men. But in the biblical and Christian view of humanity, that is precisely true. Women do need men. Men do need women. They need each other so much that when a man and woman are joined together they become the complementary halves of a new thing—"one flesh," the nucleus of a family, a joined couple that by the grace of God is more than the sum of its parts. They become one.

This truth is at the core of creation. It is "in the beginning." It is the foundation of Christian marriage. It is, according to the Lord's teaching, the foundation for lifetime marriage without divorce. It is also profoundly obvious. Just look at the evidence. The way a man's body *fits* a woman's suggests that their complementarity is deeply rooted in their natures. But they are complementary in other ways also—psychological, social, spiritual. This is almost too obvious to mention. And yet it is still difficult for some people to understand. Many leaders of more or less anti-Christian thinking in modern culture are in a wildly irrational state of denial about this basic truth of human nature: that men and women are different. That is often because they think of marriage as a cultural custom, or a legal arrangement, or an agreement for sexual comfort and economic convenience—a mere human invention.

Whatever the cause of their failure to understand, the teaching of Jesus is clearly opposed to the shallow understanding of sexuality that pervades our culture. The Son of God teaches that marriage is the profound joining, both physical and spiritual, of a man and woman. It is so profound that they cannot be separated after marriage. Those who choose marriage therefore find that this intimate and permanent union is what their sexuality *means*.[5] This is the "nuptial meaning" of the body, as Pope John Paul II teaches. And as that meaning is an essential ingredient of what it means to be human, there can be no separation of the body and its functions from the true self. The complementarity of the sexes, and the consequent opportunity for a man and a woman actually to become "one" in a lifelong sacramental union, are truths that lie at the heart of human nature.

Living in such a union is a great challenge. But God never asks the impossible of us. The Holy Father teaches that married couples, strengthened by prayer and the sacraments of the Eucharist and Reconciliation, will be able to keep alive their awareness of the unique influence that the grace of the sacrament of marriage has on every aspect of married life, including therefore their sexuality: the gift of the Spirit, accepted and responded to by husband and wife, helps them to live their human sexuality in accordance with God's plan and as a sign of the unitive and fruitful love of Christ for His Church.[6]

Sexual morality in marriage—or, marital chastity. I stated in Chapter 1 that all human beings are obligated to be chaste. Chastity should not be confused with celibacy. For priests or nuns, who have vowed to abstain from sexual activity, celibacy and chastity are the same. For married people, however, chastity doesn't usually involve celibacy. Everything said here about sexual morality is about *chastity in marriage.*

Sexuality is a defining part of human nature. Since this is so, its moral expression is very important in determining our success as human beings. If we fail to be moral sexually, we fail to succeed as human beings. The norms by which we adhere to our higher nature (this is really what morality is about) are necessarily very important indeed. That is why the Scriptures, and Christ, and the Church led in faith by the apostles and guided through the ages by the Holy Spirit, all condemn sexual practices that debase the human person. For these practices lead not only to a failure of life for those who engage in them, but to an *eternal failure in separation from God.* This is how important the matter is. Don't listen to those shrill voices that say God doesn't care very much what we do sexually. It is Satan who says that sex is no big deal.

Those who come to the Catholic Church for blessing of their marriage should also understand without fail that the moral norms taught by the Church are far more than a set of "rules" like the rules for a game. In fact, in her moral teaching the Church herself rarely gives orders. She points rather to the objective reality of the moral law, and to the perils of breaking it. Then she lets us make up our own minds. What we find in the case of sexual morality in marriage is therefore not a bunch of changeable rules, but a map of objective reality pointing to the great spiritual benefits of a human life lived close to the Lord. Jesus is, after all, the Way.

» Lest this chapter end vaguely, here are some of the specific sexual practices that are *absolutely* ruled out by the moral law. I mention them here because those who have led the "sexual revolution" have taught our culture that these practices are all right. But they are not:

• *Adultery.* I here mean this term in its common, modern sense. It denotes sexual relations between a married person and someone he is not married to. Adultery is a direct violation of the command: "You shall not commit adultery" (Exodus 20.14). It is therefore a direct rejection of God's word and authority. *It reflects at least a temporary rejection of one's own marital commitment.* For this reason, it is *completely incompatible* with the marital vocation and with the vows men and women take to pursue that vocation faithfully. Adultery doesn't "break" a true marriage, but it can cause a lifetime of bitterness and pain. *Only those who are truly determined to avoid even the temptation to adultery should marry.*

• *Fornication.* This is the closely related sin of sexual relations between unmarried people. I have discussed it in Chapter 2, where the incompatibility of cohabitation with preparation for marriage is clarified.

• *Masturbation.* The Church, basing her teaching on Scripture, has always maintained that masturbation is seriously sinful. Because it is *self*-oriented, it denies the complete giving of oneself to one's spouse that is necessary in marriage. Furthermore, since it is usually accompanied by adulterous sexual fantasies, it involves the *mental sin* of adultery or fornication. We must remember Jesus' teaching that merely lusting after someone is spiritually the same sin as adultery: "Every one who looks at a woman lustfully has already committed adultery with her in her heart" (Matthew 5.28). Therefore giving oneself to fantasy sexual partners is incompatible with marriage. But masturbation is wrong even without fantasies. It is wrong even when committed for some therapeutic purpose such as "relieving tension." Why? (1) Because in its very nature it is contraceptive and sterile. And (2) it involves the secession of the masturbator from the oneness of the marital union. In doing so it reasserts a false and nonmarital ownership over one's sexual functions. These functions belong to your spouse, not to you. They are given in the vows of marriage. It is an act of infidelity to take them back and direct them somewhere else, even in one's own mind. Likewise, for the unmarried, masturbation is wrong, for it militates against preparation for marriage. It violates the prohibition of Scripture and the Church. It says that sexual acts outside of marriage are okay. Finally, in so-called "mutual masturbation" the partners merely help *each other* to *secede* from the marriage. Both become mere objects for use rather than persons to be loved. This act does not accord with true human dignity. It is hardly what is meant by a "sincere gift of self."

• *Using pornography.* Like the masturbation that usually accompanies it, the use of pornography is always seriously wrong. Because it involves lust for people to whom one is not married, it is an attack on the sanctity of the marital union. What's more, like much other behavior that causes chemical changes in the brain, it is addictive. Pornography addicts never get enough of the stuff. They make poor husbands and wives because they are addicted to thinking sexually about strangers. Those strangers, in turn, are not human; they are mere objects, reduced to such by their own will. If you are in the habit of using pornography, you need to break that habit—perhaps even with the help of professional counseling—before you will be qualified to marry. Ignoring this need will throw your marriage on the rocks.

• *Contraception.* See the next chapter.

• *Abortion.* The natural child of contraception. See the next chapter.

Discussion questions

1. Does "anything go" sexually in marriage? Why or why not?
2. If chastity is equivalent to sexual morality, what can be meant by "chaste thoughts" and "chaste eyes"?
3. How does life according to God's moral law help us to grow as

human beings?

4. The union between man and woman is a true "human good." How can pornography and masturbation damage that good?

5. As a married couple, do you want to live in a sexual fantasy world with strangers or in the real world with each other?

6. Chastity is usually thought of as being negative. Why is this a narrow view? What positive aspects of chastity can you think of?

7. Is chastity the same thing as abstinence? Why?

Notes to Chapter 4

(1) Pope John Paul II, *Familiaris Consortio*, no. 32, in *Vatican II: More Postconciliar Documents*, ed. Austin Flannery (Grand Rapids, Michigan: Eerdmans, 1982). Italics added.

(2) Ibid., no. 11.

(3) Pope John Paul II, *Letter to Families*, no. 6 (Boston: St. Paul Books & Media, 1994). Italics in original.

(4) Ibid. Italics in original.

(5) See Leonard F. Gerke, *Christian Marriage: A Permanent Sacrament* (Washington: Catholic University of America Press, 1965). Fr. Gerke's book is a historical study of how permanence is an *essential* feature of the sacramentality of marriage. No permanence, no sacrament.

(6) Pope John Paul II, *Familiaris Consortio*, no. 33.

CHAPTER 5

CHILDREN

Truth and the goodness of creation. In the beginning, when God created the world, He "saw everything that He had made, and behold, it was very good" (Genesis 1.31). God was inclined by His grace to make a good universe. He then approved of it and extended His sustaining love to it. You and I and the earth, and the constellations and everything that is, exist because God approves of that existence. He loves it. This is how it is that "love makes the world go round." God created a good universe as an expression of His love, and it is His ongoing love that holds everything in being. God sends forth His Spirit, and all beings are created; when He withdraws His Spirit, they die (see Psalm 104.29-30).

It is our highest human calling to *love* genuinely. In doing so, in our own small way, we *replay* God's creative love in our own lives. For most people this calling finds expression in marriage. Marriage is "the rock on which the family is built."[1] Marital love is the human bond in which the couple's mutual love resembles the love of God within the Holy Trinity and the love of Christ for the Church.

But love between husband and wife is also like God in His creativity. God lets us share His unbounded creative love by actually bringing into existence new human beings, who are "very good" and who increase the kingdom of love and life. We call this gift *procreation.* What an honor, and what a responsibility!

The fact that creativity and love are so bonded is the origin of the Church's teaching on children. As I have stated, the union between man and woman is good in itself. Some people can't have children. But their union is still holy. Most couples, however, can and should have children. The Church taught at the Second Vatican Council (and throughout the ages before it) that children are a primary good of marriage. "Marriage and married love are by nature ordered to the procreation and education of children. Indeed children are the supreme gift of marriage and greatly contribute to the good of the parents themselves."[2] Therefore, "Married couples should regard it as their proper mission to transmit human life and to educate their children; they should realize that they are thereby cooperating with the love of God the Creator and are, in a certain sense, its interpreters."[3]

The Holy Father teaches that the "common good" of the husband and wife is realized in the birth of a child.[4] In having children the couple are "cooperating with God to call new human beings into existence" and therefore "contributing to the transmission of that divine image and likeness of which everyone 'born of a woman' is a bearer."[5] In this way God actually enables us to propagate His image in the world.

Catholic couples *must* agree to do this if they are able. To restate one of the requirements of Catholic marriage given in Chapter 1: *a man and woman who intend never to have children are denying a basic, good component of marriage and therefore cannot marry validly. An openness to having children is an essential requirement for all who want a genuine sacramental marriage.*

How many children and when? Every human being has an innate dignity given him by God. This dignity belongs to him whether any other human being wills it or not. Whether he is wanted or not, or "accidental" or not, every human being conceived has the dignity of being a human person created in God's image. This fact says a lot about the attitude a couple should have toward children. Every child is a gift beyond measure—the image of the Creator—and should be accepted as such.

The old stereotypical image of the Catholic family—with seven, ten, or twelve children—is not often encountered in real life any more. And that's a pity. Western culture has become more and more materialistic, and the individuals who live in it have become more and more *afraid* and *selfish*. This is what it boils down to. This is what all the palaver about "overpopulation" really means. It is rare to find a couple with the courage to have a large family.

We should make no mistake about it: courage and trust in God are the needed elements. The Second Vatican Council taught:

> Whenever Christian spouses in a spirit of sacrifice and trust in divine providence carry out their duties of procreation with generous human and Christian responsibility, they glorify the Creator and perfect themselves in Christ. Among the married couples who thus fulfill their God-given mission, special mention should be made of those who after

prudent reflection and common decision courageously undertake the proper upbringing of a large number of children.[6]

There are serious leaders in the Catholic Church today who say that the best thing Catholic couples can do to improve the future of society is to have *large* families and raise them in the fear and love of God.

However, couples have a choice. The Church recognizes that no single rule about family size will serve for all people. Couples may find that they need to limit the number of children they have. They also may find it important for the good of the family as a whole to space births out, so that the duties of taking care of infants are spread over a number of years.

Moral theologians of the highest caliber—indeed, the Holy Father Himself —recognize that couples have a large number of variables to consider when planning a family. Different social and economic factors, different life experiences, different capabilities—all can rightly influence the decision whether to have a child now or to wait. It is very important to know that the Church approves of such planning. At the very least, the individual conscience, *if rightly formed,* can lead to a correct moral decision. It may be very important for the economic, social, or psychological welfare of the couple to wait for the next pregnancy. A family may already be as large as the parents can hope to handle.

The final consideration, however, is this: *married couples should not postpone pregnancy without a good reason. And they should never, under any circumstances, adopt the idea underlying the modern, contraceptive mentality—that children are an enemy of their wellbeing. As a Catholic, you must form your conscience in accord with the teaching of the Church.*

One thing to remember: merely wanting to be at ease, not wanting to be bothered, wanting only to live in a bigger house than you need or drive a better car, is not a sufficient reason to postpone a pregnancy. You must bring to bear on such moral decisions all of the important relevant features. These include the wellbeing of the existing children, your income, perhaps your desire to devote yourself solely to the current baby's development. But you must always remember that, as the Holy Father teaches in his *Letter to Fami-*

lies, the only human act that has real merit is a "sincere gift of self."[7] Do not let your decision be based on selfish motives. *Giving yourself away*—to spouse, to children, to serving the needy, to work in the Church—is the only way of achieving true human development or finding true joy in life. For this was the course of Christ's life. Our Lord gave Himself to others from the time of the Annunciation to His death on the cross. Married or single, if you want to save your life, you will have to give it away.

Human dignity, contraception, and the Church. So faithful Catholic teachers acknowledge that it is sometimes a good idea to postpone pregnancy. *But they also teach that it is absolutely necessary to do this in a morally acceptable way.* We must understand the Church's teaching about *permissible* ways of spacing births. And that brings us to one of the most controversial battlegrounds of the "culture wars"—the field of conflict between contraception and natural family planning. Most people in our society are deluded about the false threat of "overpopulation." Such people are blind to the fact that the developed world is now facing a catastrophic *de*population. They are also increasingly devoted to materialism and pleasure. These facts help them decide that contraception is not only okay but necessary. The rightness of contraception is hardly ever questioned in our society at large.

You should understand that the Catholic Church teaches that contraception is always wrong. It is contrary to human development. It is contrary to true self-giving in marriage. It is destructive. The Church teaches this solemnly, and that teaching is not going to change.

The historical record of the harm of contraception should enlighten us. At the beginning of the twentieth century the divorce rate was very low—in single digits. Divorce was generally confined to people in show biz. Among ordinary people a divorced person was both an oddity and an outcast. In 1930, however, the Anglican Church decreed that contraception was morally acceptable. Until that time, *all* churches had taught that it was immoral. This fact is worth repeating: *all Christian churches agreed, and had agreed for nearly 2,000 years, that contraception is wrong.* After the disastrous Anglican decision, the idea of being "liberated" from fertility festered until, by the end of the 1960s, most mainline Christians accepted contraception as moral. *The divorce rate climbed right along with contraception.*

The Catholic Church, however, knowing that the moral law is not subject to change by human decree, continued to teach the truth. But large numbers of Catholics, lured by false freedoms, expected the Church to change her teaching. Their disappointment, scandalously shared and expressed by numerous priests, broke into open rebellion after 1968, when Pope Paul VI solemnly taught in *Humanae Vitae* that the moral law regarding contraception had not changed and could not be changed. That pivotal decade, the 1960s, marked a sharp turn upward in the divorce rate, even, as we have said, among Catholics.

One of the gravest mistakes in human thinking is the widespread idea that dignity or worth is given by human beings. We are led to believe, for instance, that *wanting* a baby confers *value* on it; if we don't confer that value, the child is worthless. So "unwanted" children in the womb can be destroyed. Or we redefine the term "human being" to exclude those we object to—unborn children, senile people, disabled people, or some other classification. Once we decide that human dignity depends upon human judgment, there is no limit to the number of human beings that can be *excluded* from our vision of a high-quality life. When the Supreme Court stupidly decided some decades ago that it didn't know what a "person" is, it left the definition of this term up for grabs.

The Church, however, following the lead of her Master, has always taught:

- That human worth comes from a supernatural and not a human source.
- That all human beings are created in the image of God.
- That all human beings, born and unborn, are unique and irreplaceable individuals, endowed by God with a value, a dignity that cannot be given by man or taken away by him.

It is the denial of this great truth that has enabled our "culture of death"[8] to take such firm hold on our minds. Now, to our shame, we pay garden-variety atheists and nihilists to teach "ethics" to our children in prestigious universities. *The innate dignity of human beings is the value behind the following discussion of contracep-*

tion. Indeed, it is behind the whole moral law, which requires us to act as befits human persons. The call to act in accord with genuine human dignity challenges our weaknesses and social evils and demands of us real human growth. This growth clearly exhibits the image of our Creator.

You should understand that this discussion, even more than some other parts of this brief book, offers only a general look at the Church's teaching. For a deeper look, see the works listed at the end of the book.

» *Some immoral features of contraception:*

• Contraception is beneath human dignity.

God gives great worth to every human being, *as a human being.* But part of the human nature created by God is the responsibility to act in accord with that worth. That too belongs to us as a species. When we in effect say to each other, "I love you but only if you're chemically sterilized at the time," we attack the integrity of God's creation and deny each other's dignity. *That is not love.* When we treat ourselves like animals, we act beneath our dignity. *That is not love.* More subtly, when a man says to a woman, "I want you on the pill so we won't have to worry about your getting pregnant," he is saying in effect, "I love you but not the you that God created. I love only an altered version of you. I reject the part of you that most deeply characterizes your feminine nature." *That is not love.* More subtly still, whenever people decide to use contraception, they abandon the control of reason and give themselves over to control of their hormones. Indeed, this is the very purpose of their taking contraceptives. They don't want to "worry," i.e., think and control themselves. *That too is not love, but abandonment of reason.* You will note that the part of man created in God's image is precisely his ability to think and control himself. When we abandon it, we reject God's image and become controlled by something lower. We act in rebellion against our true human nature.

• *Contraception is also beneath the dignity of Matrimony.*

As we have seen, those who marry are called to a genuine sacramental union, which involves above all a "sincere gift of self."[9] But *this gift is sincere because it is a gift of our whole selves as we are, not as people whose procreative gift is removed by surgery or pills.*

There is all the difference in the world between limiting births through *cooperation* with God's creation, and limiting them through an end run around that creation. Those who dissent from the Church's teaching on contraception—whether priests, theologians, or laity—either don't see this or think it's no big deal. These people are feeding the divorce courts. They are attacking the very concept of the family. You should pray for them and dare to be different.

• *Contraception is physically destructive.*

In addition to its opposition to the marital commitment, contraception is physically destructive. Birth-control pills have lasting ill effects on a woman's health. The details about these are beyond the scope of this book. (See the suggestions for further reading.) But perhaps worst of all, *birth-control pills of all kinds cause abortions.* That is, when the circumstances are right, they are not "contraceptive" at all, but abortifacient. This book does not discuss abortion much. But all Catholics who have even the slightest regard for the teachings of the Church know that abortion is among the gravest moral offenses that can be committed. Here's how the pill works: If it fails to prevent fertilization of the ovum, as often happens, it causes the destruction of the young human being who has been conceived. Women who are on birth-control pills generally abort one child a year. Think about it. Do you want to do that?

• *Contraception has contributed to cultural decline.*

As long ago as Pope Pius XI, the leaders of the Catholic Church were warning against the bad consequences that would follow the acceptance of contraception. In his answer to the Anglican edict that contraception is okay, the Holy Father wrote: "any use whatsoever of *Matrimony* exercised in such a way that the act is *deliberately frustrated in its natural power* to generate life is an offense against the law of God and of nature, and those who indulge in such are branded with the guilt of a grave sin."[10] He reflected on the fact that this Church teaching:

•• developed from ancient revelation

•• was expressed by St. Augustine as long ago *as the fourth century*

•• and has never changed.

Some of the results that the Pope foresaw if people started using contraception were:

- •• an increase in fornication and adultery,
- •• an increase in the killing of unborn children,
- •• and an increase in divorce.

Nothing could be clearer than this: Pope Pius XI was exactly right in his predictions. Since 1930 the divorce rate has risen from less than 10 percent to more than 50 percent. For people who live together and contracept before marriage, the failure rate is 70 percent.[11]

Pope Paul VI reaffirmed the moral law in 1968. He did so in what has become the most important single Church document of modern times, *Humanae Vitae.* This is a wonderful work about the beauty of human sexuality. *You should read it, carefully and with prayer.* But it has also been viciously attacked precisely because it affirmed the Church's teaching. When it came out, many Catholics, even priests, denounced it. As a result, many Catholics have abandoned the Church's moral teaching and taken up contraception. *As a result, the Catholic divorce rate has risen to everyone else's level.* This is the effect of rejecting the moral law. Marriages are just as troubled in the Catholic Church as elsewhere. Public approval of fornication, adultery, and abortion has likewise grown dramatically. Contraception is directly linked to all these evils. It has contributed to widespread:

- •• *sexual immorality*
- •• *marital breakup*
- •• *and killing of innocent human beings.*

You can't control everyone else. But you have the power to do something about this problem in your marriage. I pray with all my heart that you will make the right decision and stick with it faithfully.

The moral solution. Marital failure has become the norm, thanks in part to contraception. But you fortunately have a choice. That choice is *natural family planning.* Natural family planning is based on a combination of self-knowledge and self-control. It teaches that a couple can avoid a pregnancy by knowing when the woman is fertile and avoiding intercourse at that time. Note that this method is not contraception. For though a couple who use natural family planning might want to wait to have a child, they do not alter themselves chemically, mechanically, or surgically to avoid pregnancy. They also do not engage in onanism or sodomy, sins that are becoming increasingly popular. Their sexual union is still *open* to the conception of a child, although conception may be extremely unlikely by their own choice. In other words, they totally accept the bodies that God gave them, control their activities with the minds that God gave them, and thus cooperate with God's creation. They also know that every human child is a great blessing.

» *The rewards of natural family planning are great:*
- A husband and wife who learn to use it also learn to have a deep knowledge of each other as images of God.
- A corresponding profound respect for each other is a natural result.
- The practice of natural family planning is a *mutual* enterprise for which both husband and wife are responsible. It enriches their cooperation in life.

No more anger against the wife because she didn't take her pill. No more stealth pregnancies. *This deep collaboration is part of the true sacrament of marriage.*

I heard a priest ask not long ago what there was about natural family planning couples that makes them so attractive and serene. The answer is that NFP users have a peace and harmony in their lives that comes from a deep acceptance of and cooperation with God's good creation. Others cooperate with pharmaceutical companies and misguided doctors in order to thwart their own nature. In a sense they *avoid* each other, indeed avoid themselves, while seeking unlimited access to orgasms. Theirs is a schizophrenic process. It leads to marriages in which *neither partner is actually present,* both having rejected and diminished themselves as God made them. No wonder contraceptors divorce so often. And, on the other hand, no wonder users of natural family planning have such a low divorce rate. They accept their own nature and cooperate with it instead of warring against it.

What *is* the divorce rate for couples who faithfully practice natural family planning? I have heard statistics ranging from less than 1 percent to 11 percent. Whichever it is, consider this startling fact: *for those who practice natural family planning, the divorce rate is about the same as it was in 1910!*

>*Two more things:*
 • First, *natural family planning is* not *"calendar rhythm."*
 People not familiar with natural family planning are almost perverse in their insistence that those "idiot Catholics" are still stuck on the "rhythm method" of family planning. They seem to have sworn to remain ignorant. Most of the press, ever alert, wallows in this ignorance and tries to spread it. But there is no real resemblance between natural family planning and the rhythm method. *The rhythm method is based on crude guesses and doesn't work. It assumes falsely that all women are alike in their menstrual cycles. NFP is based on self-knowledge. It is not only moral, it works.*
 Natural family planning is based on a couple's *real knowledge* of when the woman ovulates. This cannot be achieved by looking at a calendar and guessing. It can, however, be achieved with complete success by means that anyone can learn. *When you learn about natural family planning, you will learn more about what a miracle your body is than you have previously imagined.* You will learn why *Humanae Vitae* is such a beautiful, important document. And you will be able to regulate pregnancy as effectively as with any other means, including the poisonous Pill.
 • Second, *natural family planning works both ways.*
 If you want to become pregnant and have trouble doing so, NFP can help you. Many of the "fertility drugs" given to infertile couples can be avoided by the use of natural family planning. And many of the morally objectionable procedures used by fertility doctors will no longer seem necessary.
 In conclusion, one of the best things you can do for your coming marriage is to resolve right now that you will be faithful to the Church's teaching on contraception. Find teachers of natural family planning, through your Catholic diocese or through other means such as the yellow pages. (Look under "Abortion Alternatives." But beware of snakes: Planned Parenthood, the largest abortion profiteer in the world, also has a listing there. So do other abortionists, whose "alternative" to abortion is contraceptives.) *Attend a natural family planning premarital session.* If the clergyman supervising your marriage preparation insists on this, you are blessed. If not, do it anyway. Your priest or deacon probably knows who teaches natural family planning near you. Further, get a book on

the subject and read it (some are listed at the end of this book). Really *learn* about it before you even consider rejecting it. Finally, find a family doctor who supports natural family planning. Such courageous doctors are a great blessing, and they are increasing in number.

Discussion questions

1. Are you both agreed on the matter of having children—both when and how many?

2. Do you both accept the Church's teaching on contraception and natural family planning? Do you realize how serious a difference of opinion in this matter would be?

3. The Holy Trinity is the source of all union, or communion, or harmonious relationship between people. In what ways does contraceptive sex fail to reflect this union?

4. How truly Catholic are nominal Catholics who accept and advocate abortion?

5. Do you think our moral and philosophical development has kept up with our technological development? Why?

Notes to chapter 5

(1) This is the title of an excellent book on marriage by a leading moral theologian: William E. May, *Marriage: The Rock on Which the Family is Built* (San Francisco: Ignatius Press, 1995).

(2) Vatican II, *Gaudium et Spes (Pastoral Constitution on the Church in the Modern World)*, no. 50, in *Documents of Vatican II*, ed. Austin Flannery (Northport, New York: Costello, 1975).

(3) Loc. cit.

(4) See Pope John Paul II, *Letter to Families,* no. 11 (Boston: St. Paul Books & Media, 1994).

(5) Ibid., no. 8.

(6) *Gaudium et Spes,* no. 50.

(7) Pope John Paul II, *Letter to Families,* no. 11.

(8) See Pope John Paul II's wonderful encyclical letter on the "culture of life," *Evangelium Vitae (The Gospel of Life)* (1997).

(9) Pope John Paul II, *Letter to Families,* no. 11.

(10) Pope Pius XI, *Casti Connubii* (December 31, 1930), no. 56. Italics added.

(11) Michael J. McManus, "Veil of Tears," *Policy Review,* Winter 1994.

Journey of Faith:

CHAPTER 6

MODELS OF THE FAMILY

I now turn to a comparative discussion of different concepts of the family. Our understanding of family life will determine how our family functions. What we think a family really is or should be will have a lot to do with the kind of family we form. It is therefore important to clarify the Catholic concept of family. This concept has cultural aspects, but it also transcends the laws of all countries and times.

The concept of family is broader than marriage but built on it. For some decades the family unit itself has been the topic of much earnest concern in the Church. This is because the family as an institution has been weakened by divorce and other evils, especially in the affluent countries of the West. In the United States, Germany, Britain, France, the Netherlands, and other Western nations, the divorce courts have grown fat on anti-Christian fare. This includes adultery, contraception, abortion, fear of "over-population," and plain self-worship.

The idea of easy, "no-fault" divorce has accelerated the problem. Social ills have grown rapidly as a result. The connection of divorce to our worst social problems has become clear. Let no one misunderstand me. I love and respect single mothers and fathers. They do heroic work. We must see Jesus in them and help them as much as possible. But this doesn't mean that single parenthood is good in itself. Crime soars with the predominance of single-parent families, which are produced by divorce. Further single-parented children in turn produce more single-parent families, which produce more ill-guided young people. Despite the promises of their advocates, contraceptives have played a major role in fanning this flame to a blaze that is consuming the inner cities of America and spreading everywhere else. The illusion that condoms and pills will avert further evil is just that: an illusion.

Against such a situation the Church holds up the vocation to genuine family life. Here is what the Second Vatican Council had to say about the subject:

> The mission of being the primary vital cell of society has been given to the family by God Himself. This mission will be accomplished if the family, by the mutual affection of its members and by family prayer, presents itself as a domestic sanctuary of the Church; if the whole family takes its part in the Church's liturgical worship; if, finally, it offers active hospitality, and practices justice and other good works for the benefit of all its brothers suffering from want.[1]

This is a high calling. But it is not out of our reach. The family advocated by the Church is not an unattainable ideal of peace and harmony. *You* can form such a family.

Having had more experience in human affairs than any other organization in history, the Church teaches the truth without illusion. She does not teach that family life can be free of conflict. She teaches, rather, that the family is the social unit in which:

- conflicts can *best* be resolved
- individuals can be raised to develop their human potential to the *fullest* extent
- society finds its *best* hope for the future.

Among Christians, however, the reality of family life has sometimes fallen short of Christian teaching. Surely we all do that, both individually and collectively. No one is perfect. Nevertheless, we recognize that family life has declined in our time. Until the antifamily movements of the twentieth century, the Christian family maintained itself by high standards for centuries. In spite of much criticism of the traditional family, does anyone really believe that family life in general is better now than it was a few decades ago? Even some secularists are coming to realize that the type of family taught by the Church is the only hope for social stability in a world that is growing increasingly unstable.

Chapter 4 is explicitly about marriage as a sacrament and vocation. Here I want to put the sacramental character of marriage in clearer perspective by contrasting the Catholic concept of marriage with other concepts. The essential character of Christian marriage is not well understood in modern Western cultures. It has been obscured or even replaced by inferior, competing concepts of the structure of marriage. The most important of these distorted, false concepts are 1) the civil-contract model of marriage and 2) the master-servant model. I discuss these in order to clarify the proper Christian understanding of marriage: 3) the sacramental-community model.

The civil-contract model. As its name implies, the civil-contract model treats marriage as a secular enterprise. According to this concept, marriages should be patterned on business contracts and other legal agreements. In this model, marriage receives its sanction from the government. The essence of marriage, according to radical secularists and statists, is an agreement entered into with the government's permission. The sign of this permission is called a license. Just as the government licenses qualified people to drive or sell poultry or hot dogs, it licenses people to marry.

With government control, however, comes government power. If the government defines the concept of marriage, it has the power to *redefine* the institution without any reference to God, the Scriptures, or the natural law. We currently see a lot of misguided efforts based on this false freedom. Appeals on the part of homosexuals for sanction of their unions as "marriages," for instance, depend upon the presumption that marriage is wholly a creature of the government. They think that all we need to make a homosexual union into a "marriage" is a new government definition. This presumption is also behind the idea that marriage can be ended with a simple no-fault lawsuit. Marriage as defined and authorized by the government is not permanent. It is just a legal arrangement. Just as it begins with a legal paper, it can end with one. Thus marriage, separated from its origin in God's good creation, has been debased in our culture.

But note this: *None* of the civil-contract model of marriage as such is in accord with divine revelation. That is because:

- The essence of marriage is not a civil agreement but a divinely sanctioned covenant.
- Marriages do not receive their validity from any government license but from the mutual commitment of the couple in the sight of God.
- A real marriage is permanent. In the eyes of God, divorce is as much a legal fiction as a merely civil marriage.

Journey of Faith:

Of course, in a pluralist society such as ours the government has to be involved in marriage. We need government to give married couples and their children tax breaks, for instance, and thereby encourage the formation of families. This is cooperation with natural law. But governments far overreach their rightful authority when they presume to redefine marriage and make it a flimsy and fleeting, secular arrangement.

Here is an extremely simplified and partial account of how the civil-contract model of marriage came to be in the Western world. It originated in the Protestant movement of the sixteenth century. Until that time, the Catholic Church had been solely in charge of marriage. Marriage, after all, is a sacrament, and sacraments are administered by the Church. Secularizing tendencies received a great boost from King Henry VIII of England, who didn't like his wife and wanted to marry a little cutey that he had noticed hanging around the royal court. (He later cut off her cute head.) When the Church refused to let him dispose of his wife, he proclaimed himself head of the Church in England so that he could do what he wanted. Thus explicitly rejecting the Church's authority over the sacrament of Matrimony, he grasped that authority for himself. In doing so, he started a new religious body opposed to the Catholic Church. Sad to say, almost all of the English bishops proved themselves more loyal to the government than to God by going along with the king. That the sacraments are found only in the Church had proved a problem to Henry.

The sacraments also posed a problem for others who broke with Catholicism. Without the priesthood, how could they continue to receive the other sacraments, since these came only from priests in union with the Holy Father? Over time, they arrived at a simple enough answer: Without sacraments you don't need priests. Many Protestant communions therefore denied the very concept of a sacrament mediated by the Church and claimed to turn to the Bible alone for sanction of their practices. This dispensed once and for all with the Church's authority over marriage. Still, marriage had to be regulated by *some* authority. That authority turned out to be the government.

Nevertheless, for the next several centuries virtually all Christian communions retained the ancient, Catholic, Scriptural understanding that marriage came from God, was sanctioned by Christ, and was permanent. The idea that government should have sole authority came slowly. Not until the twentieth century—which witnessed a reckless turn against marriage and family—did the civil-contract concept of marriage become the norm in western culture.

The results have not been good. Among them, as I have said, has been an explosion of single-parent families that brought with it many social evils, including an epidemic of crime committed by fatherless boys. The intact family, consisting of a father, a mother, and their children, became a relic of the past.

This relic is a Christian *sign of contradiction,* a declaration against false progress and societal disintegration. Couples who marry in the Catholic Church should strive to be such a sign, which declares that truth is not subject to changes in taste and legal presumption. *If you are called to Catholic marriage, you are called to be a living sign of contradiction to the prevailing concept of marriage, which is the civil-contract model.*

The master-servant model. The civil-contract model of marriage has no Scriptural warrant or sanction in Church history. By contrast, the *master-servant concept* of marriage has been widely considered to be authorized, indeed commanded, by Scripture. But this interpretation of Scripture is not adequate. In a true marriage, the husband is not the master, and the wife is not his servant. They are servants of each other. The husband is the "head," but only as Christ is the Head of the Church. Let us clarify this.

In Chapter 1 was quoted part of a passage of major importance about marriage from the writings of St. Paul. Here is the passage in full:

> Be subject to one another out of reverence for Christ. Wives, be subject to your husbands, as to the Lord. For the husband is the head of the wife as Christ is the head of the Church, His body, and is Himself its Savior. As the Church is subject to Christ, so let wives also be subject in everything to their husbands. Husbands, love your wives, as Christ loved the Church and gave Himself up for her, that He might sanctify her, having cleansed her by the washing of water with the word, that He might present the Church to Himself in splendor, without spot or wrinkle or any such thing, that she might

> be holy and without blemish. Even so husbands should love
> their wives as their own bodies. He who loves his wife loves
> himself. For no man ever hates his own flesh, but nourishes
> and cherishes it, as Christ does the Church, because we are
> members of His body. "For this reason a man shall leave his
> father and mother and be joined to his wife, and the two
> shall become one." This a great mystery, and I mean in ref-
> erence to Christ and the Church; however, let each one of
> you love his wife as himself, and let the wife see that she
> respects her husband (Ephesians 5.21-33).

Countless millions of Christians have taken this passage and others similar to it as authorization of a master-servant concept of
marriage. Countless millions of successful, even quite happy marriages and families have resulted. At the same time, an untold number of marriages have been marred by a domestic tyranny falsely
based on the words of St. Paul. The failure to read the words "Wives,
be subject to your husbands" in the context of the *whole* passage
has led countless men to treat their wives as lowly servants, even to
consider this mistreatment as good, Scriptural, and Christian. Such
treatment is difficult to reconcile with genuine love. There is no
true warrant for the master-servant idea in this passage or in any
other passage of the New Testament.

» **Just what idea of marriage *does* the passage present?**

• Any answer true to the text will acknowledge that the relation between a Christian husband and his wife is mysterious.

St. Paul clearly states that the reality of marriage is a "great mystery." We can explore this mystery as far as the difficult words of
Scripture allow, but no further. St. Paul himself seems baffled by
the revealed truth.

• Still, there can be no doubt that St. Paul prescribes a model
of marriage in which the husband is the head of the family.

Many readers of this passage, often infected with radical feminism, reject the idea that there is any kind of authority structure in
marriage. But they are wrong. The Church, relying on St. Paul as a
fount and origin of Christian teaching on marriage, has always accepted this scriptural teaching: the husband is head of the wife,
head of the family.

This famous reading teaches both *mutual subjection* and *headship.* Both of these are essential and binding on us. Neither is "culturally conditioned," and neither can be thrown out. If the husband isn't the head of the wife in marriage, as St. Paul teaches, then the analogy with Christ and the Church doesn't work. But it does work, and beautifully. Jesus, the Head of the Church, loves His Bride to the extent that He totally sacrifices Himself to her. While she—one flesh with him, as husband and wife are one flesh—is sanctified by her intimacy with Him. As the Good Shepherd, He gives His life for the sheep. As the Groom, He gives His life, even his body and blood, to His Bride. He even gives His Spirit to her, and considers Himself bound by her decisions. Now *that* is mutual subjection, and it is by no means negated by Christ's headship.

But just what does this mean in practical terms? What implications does it have for a hierarchy of authority in marriage? I have known outspoken Christian husbands, in avidly Christian families, who couldn't converse with their wives for five minutes without saying who was boss. I have known wives who earned all the money in the family but still had to ask their husbands before spending a quarter. Surely this is wrong. This is certainly not the kind of arrangement that St. Paul advocates. There is no boss in the passage from St. Paul, and there is no underling. Furthermore, the idea of a boss-underling or master-servant relationship is *incompatible* with the rest of the description of marriage.

- Then *how* is the husband head of the wife? *As Christ is head of the Church.*

Does Jesus exert the power of a boss over the Church? Certainly not. His mission, Scripture tells us, was summed up in *service*, not in dictatorial authority. "The Son of man . . . came not to be served but to serve, and to give His life as a ransom for many" (Mark 10.45). The "many" are the Church. So the relation between Christ and the Church is one of self-effacement, self-gift, self-sacrifice. On her side, the Church is loving and submissive. She knows her Head. But the bawling master of the house, who will tolerate no disobedience, who tries to rule not only the decisions but even the thoughts of his family, is entirely absent from the Pauline model of marriage.

The sacramental-community model. Now for the Catholic concept. In contrast to the master-servant model, a genuine Catholic marriage constitutes a sacramental community of love.

• This is a relationship in which husband and wife are *subject to one another and bring Christ to one another.*

This is, to be sure, something of a paradox: the husband is "head" of the wife and yet is subject to her, as she is subject to him. *"Be subject to one another* out of reverence for Christ," St. Paul says. This mandate surely precedes considerations of authority.

It has been rightly said that if a marriage is to succeed, the husband and wife must not concentrate on their so-called rights—that is, on a fifty-fifty division of authority. They must instead *defer* to one another as each would defer to Christ. This is the essence of a loving relationship. In a Christian marriage Christ truly operates sacramentally through each partner, making Himself present to a man through his wife and to a woman through her husband. That is how marriage is a sacrament—a sacramental community—and how each partner is a *minister* of that sacrament.

Older forms of the marriage ceremony often included a promise on the part of the bride to "love, honor, and obey" the husband. In recent times that word *obey* has been dropped, on the grounds that it expresses an unacceptable degree of servility. I wouldn't mind seeing the promise put back into the ceremony, but for *both* partners in the marriage. The husband and wife should promise to "love, honor, and obey" each other. What else does "be subject to each other" mean?

• This is a relationship of love *modeled on and embodying the love of God. This is the heart of St. Paul's teaching: mutual subjection in love.*

The mysterious relation between marriage and the Church, however, remains. We don't fully know how Christ rules the Church, though we know that He does so through love and not coercion. We don't fully know how Christ and the Church are one, though we see that the Church, in the administration of the sacraments, is one with her divine Lord. Christ acts *personally* through the priest at the altar and in the confessional. Likewise, we don't fully know how a husband and wife are one, but we see the analogy with the Church, for Jesus is made present and active through the ministry of husband and wife—just as He is made present at the altar by the priest.

But even if we don't fully comprehend these matters, which were a "great mystery" to St. Paul, the Lord invites couples marrying in His Church to *accept* the analogy between the Church and marriage and try to live up to it. With faith in His word, we know that Christ is made present by a Christian husband to his wife, and by a Christian wife to her husband. From this fact flow mutual esteem, mutual submission, mutual love.

Discussion questions

1. How is Christ the Head of the Church? When He gives the Church the power of "binding and loosing," what does this say about marriage?
2. What dangers does an emphasis on "rights" pose for a married couple?
3. What is the relationship between love and duty?
4. Why does the Church teach that the family is the primary social unit?
5. Do you think that the traditional "nuclear family" has value? Why?
6. So what's wrong with single parenthood? Haven't several rich single Hollywood actresses shown us that it's okay?

Notes to Chapter 6

(1) Vatican II, *Decree on the Apostolate of Lay People (Apostolicam Actuositatem)*, no. 11, in *Documents of Vatican II*, ed. Austin P. Flannery (Northport, New York: Costello, 1975).

Journey of Faith:

CHAPTER 7

FAMILY DYNAMICS

The preceding chapter discussed various models of marriage. In all of the models the husband and wife had specific roles with relation to each other. These roles are:

- civil-contract maker
- boss
- servant
- member of a sacramental community.

We have seen that the civil-contract model and the boss-servant model are defective. The sacramental-community model, on the other hand, is the "shape" of marriage taught by the Church. In this chapter I carry the topic further, to include Church teaching on:

- •• the various roles within the family
- •• the nature of authority
- •• the extended family
- •• the family as a "domestic Church," and
- •• decision-making and the resolution of conflict.

Catholic teaching on all of these topics is derived from the principal Christian mandate, which is to *"love one another"* (John 13.34). Any interpersonal thoughts, words, and actions that don't proceed from this principle or that conflict with it are not Christian. Period. From taking this command seriously, as we must do if we want to be followers of Christ, various responsibilities follow. That is because *real love is a durable devotion of the will to the true good of another person.* Love makes us responsible for pursuing that good. We do this out of gratitude to God, who pursues *our* good.

Structure and authority. A basic practical rule that specifies how a husband and a wife are to love each other is stated by St. Paul in a passage from Ephesians discussed in the preceding chapter: *"Be subject to one another out of reverence for Christ"* (Ephesians 5.21). This subjection implies a deliberate renunciation of authority. Husband defers to wife, and wife defers to husband, both in mutual respect—because they love each other. As a result of that love they honor each other and desire each other's genuine good.

The "authority structure" in a Christian marriage is therefore based largely upon authority *renounced*—given away—to one's spouse. The Holy Father teaches that the wife respects the husband

> because she loves [him] and knows that she is loved in return. It is because of this love that husband and wife *become a mutual gift.* Love contains the acknowledgment of the personal dignity of the other . . . . Each of them, however, by a conscious and responsible act, makes a free gift of self to the other and to the children received from the Lord.[1]

Problems of "getting along" in marriage, including problems of authority, result from a deficiency of love. *If you want your marriage to be a success, resolve to defer to your spouse habitually.* Make decisions on the basis of *mutual* respect. *Honor* each other's feelings and desires, likes and dislikes—because you *love* each other.

When you do that, you won't need to worry much about who is in charge. The context of genuine love and mutual subjection will make crucial decisions about disputed matters seem easy. *Someone* will occasionally have to give in, maybe reluctantly, but that act of self-giving will not constitute a loss. Deferring to your spouse's will does not hurt your dignity.

• *The role of husband and father.*

After the husband and wife have become the "nucleus" of a family with children, the vital role of the *husband and father* becomes clear. As I have said, many of the biggest evils of our society are directly proportional to the failure of fathers to fulfill their role in the family. These include the rampages of teenage gangs, drug abuse, and violent crime. Absent fathers are a major cause of these.

The father's role is a natural one, created by God. The Pope writes, "Love for his wife as mother of their children and love for the children themselves are for the man the natural way of understanding and fulfilling his own fatherhood."[2] Without that loving *presence*, "psychological and moral imbalance and notable difficulties in family relationships" develop. If a father doesn't fulfill his responsibility to be present and self-giving to his family, those problems usually called dysfunctions will develop. That fact has become much clearer in recent decades, as the percentage of families headed by an unmarried mother has grown. Such families, and their mothers, need all the help they can get from the Church and society. We must pray for them and help them all we can. But this special need in itself clearly suggests that a problem exists.

Prospective husbands and fathers who read this book should also understand that the problems of fatherless youth don't occur only in ghettoes, but also in affluent circumstances. That is because the need of a mother and her children for the husband and father is universal and natural. We cannot escape it, for it is a part of what God has made. The rash of well-publicized, wealthy, show-biz women having children without husbands is spreading like a disease. At the same time, new studies are showing the necessity of the traditional family. I fear for the rich and famous "single moms" one sees on the covers of magazines. If those women are capable of learning, they will someday regret their disregard of the need for normal family life. Most of the readers of this book are not millionaires. They should also pay heed.

(A parenthetical explanation is in order here. Women at the heads of families are often models in their self-sacrificing family leadership. They deserve love and respect. Society should try to make it possible for them both to make a living and to care for their children. The Church and other channels of help should lend assistance in raising and educating the children, especially in teaching them how to be responsible adults and to avoid seeking the deceptive comforts of gangs, drugs, and other wrong choices. But this is difficult. The very need for this kind of help means that the Church and society are trying to make up for the children's lack of responsible fathers. Single-headed households are often a reality in our society, but they are not ideal.)

So husbands and fathers must be present and responsible. At the same time, the Church teaches that their presence, though authoritative in the final analysis, must not be "oppressive." The Holy Father warns against "the phenomenon of 'machismo', or a wrong superiority of male prerogatives which humiliates women and inhibits the development of healthy family relationships."[3] The *Catechism of the Catholic Church* attributes men's "lust and domination" over women to the Fall of Man and original sin.[4] Chapter 6 of this book has characterized marriage with a macho man as an extreme example of the "boss-servant" marriage. A husband who interprets his role as that of an unreasonable, super-masculine boss *cannot* be the kind of loving husband and father described by St. Paul. Much more likely—indeed, perhaps universal among macho husbands—he will leave behind him a lifetime of ruined relationships, of pain and failure. What's more, his sons will probably grow up to be like him. Let the reader beware.

• *The role of wife and mother.*

For her part, the Second Vatican Council taught that the *wife and mother* has a natural and nurturing "central role in the home, for the children, especially the younger children, depend on her considerably."[5] Although the domestic role of women has been attacked and ridiculed in modern society, if the truth be told, it is more important than the role of the father. Even in the traditional families depicted in 1950s TV shows, the father was mainly a breadwinner and, upon special occasions, a counselor. But that role was less important than the woman's. The idea that making money to live on is more important than shaping the emotional, intellectual, and spiritual lives of young children is pure fiction. The hand that rocks the cradle still rules the world. Nevertheless, a central concept of Christian families is that *children really need both father and mother.* Single parents, both male and female, report that in their dealings with their children, they need another adult for consultation and support—an adult who loves the children as much as they do. Who could this be besides the children's own father or mother?

The Vatican Council and the Holy Father have solemnly taught that the dignity of women in marriage and in society must not be reduced. Along with their central role in the family, therefore, women are rightly concerned with "legitimate social advancement."[6] Education, jobs, and other enterprises must be open to them. At the same time, a Christian mother must never forget that her children are more important than any job or college degree. The same applies to the father. For a job or college degree is just a *thing*, and a mother's children are immortal persons for whom she is responsible. Together with her husband she is the center of the family. For both of them, this is the most important part of the vocation they have chosen by marrying. Although it is still legitimate for a Christian wife and mother to branch out *at the proper time* to appropriate roles in society, those roles are secondary to the family role. Never let anyone tell you that any job, even that of corporate head or senator or president, is more important than the role of mother.

• *Your roles as children.*

Much could be said about your own *parents* and future *in-laws* and your relation to them, but perhaps the most important points can be made in short order. Needless to say, the scriptural command to honor your parents (Exodus 20.12) still definitely applies to you. It also applies to your in-laws. Honoring your parents is not just a good idea, but a fundamental moral law. The Church and the Scriptures teach that this obligation doesn't end when the children are grown. It does, of course, change with the years, and if your parents have adjusted well to your growing up, their understanding of their authority over you has also changed. They should no longer see you as little ones needing basic protection from physical danger—from sticking screwdrivers into wall outlets, for instance, or from picking up and eating unidentified organisms. They also should no longer give you constant instruction—unless for some odd reason you have not yet learned your manners.

The chances are good that in recent years you have been less respectful of your parents' views than you might have been. Such rebellion is a part of normal growing up. But as you embark on your marriage, you should recall the respect and duty you owe to your parents. Honor is part of love. Your marriage vow will probably include a commitment to "love and honor" each other. Honor is also part of the love you owe your parents. The Holy Father makes clear, also, that parents must always strive to be worthy of honor.[7] That applies to your parents, and to you as future parents.

Ideally, the older generations are included in the Christian family so that the whole becomes, in Pope John Paul's words, a *"communion of generations,"* joined together by the "genealogy of persons."[8] This latter phrase refers to the fact that you as a person have taken your makeup from your parents. Your complex relationship with them is not just a biological one or an environmental one. It is made up, to be sure, of your genetic heritage, but also of all the years of shared experience, mutual knowledge, joys, and pains that you have been through together.

More often than one might wish, relations with parents and in-laws are not ideal. I have seen, for instance, a possessive mother who simply didn't want her son to get married *at all*, although he was fully old enough and had been going with his fiancee for many years. The mother just didn't want her son to grow up. She cried all through the wedding—not out of joy but because she wanted her son to remain a child. Chances are good that you won't encounter such a difficult psychological problem.

Let this be your rule: Count your parents and your future in-laws in on your plans, except for the ones that you and your spouse *should* keep to yourselves. Be adults to your adult parents. But don't forget that to them you are not just any adults, but their children. Keep them close to you if possible, but run your own household. Plan to help them when they need it. They have probably helped you a lot. When they are old, let them be witnesses to the "genealogy of persons"—witnesses "to the past and a source of wisdom for the young and for the future."[9] Honor them. Live in such a way that your own children will honor you.

A very important additional comment: Each of you should take the other's family very seriously. If you see problems there, remember that those problems are built into your future spouse's life. If your future mother-in-law habitually solves problems by running off to Las Vegas, that tells you something about how your spouse will solve problems. If your future father-in-law is a habitual adulterer, beware of the possibility that your future spouse may have been infected with this spiritual disease. If your future mother-in-law has habitually fled her responsibilities and problems by drinking alcohol, you should know very well that your fiancee may follow that model. Be realistic. Know who you are marrying. You are marrying a family as well as an individual. If the family is unacceptable, think again about the marriage. If there are problems, talk to each other about them until you are satisfied that they will not be a sore spot in your own marriage.

The family as a "domestic Church." If the family is the most important good thing in the married vocation, the most important aspect of the family is its spiritual life. The Church teaches that the Christian family is like the Church in important ways:

- Both were established by God, not man.
- Both are oriented toward God and dependent upon him.

• Both find unity through mutual respect among the members, through self-offering sanctified by Christ's passion, through confident assurance of forgiveness, and through an internal charity that brings spiritual healing after strife.

The Second Vatican Council and the Holy Father teach that the Christian family is a sort of miniature of the Church—a "domestic sanctuary of the Church," or a "domestic Church."[10]

The domestic Church is like the larger Church in its relation to Christ. Like the whole Church, it is the "bride of Christ" in its experience of God's love—"conjugal love, paternal and maternal love, fraternal love, the love of a community of persons and of generations."[11] The family is "grafted into the mystery of the Church to such a degree as to become a sharer . . . in the saving mission proper to the Church."[12] Just how this can be is a subject worth a great deal of study and prayer. Please give this serious thought and talk to God about it.

Here it will suffice to sketch the Churchlike functions of the family under three headings: the functions of 1) worship, 2) education, and 3) service. There is a great theological meaning here. The Holy Father teaches that these functions are aspects of what might be called the *vocation of the family*. They correspond to the roles of the Savior Himself as Priest, Prophet, and King.

• *Worship*

The Christian family is *"called to be sanctified."*[13] Like the Church, it is a worshiping community. It derives its original union from the sacraments of Baptism and *Matrimony*, both of which make Christ present to the participants. It derives its continued coherence from the Sacrifice of the Mass, and from daily development in the culture of the Church. It has its reality not just in the wedding ceremony, but in an ongoing, lifelong relationship with Christ. On that journey, the sacrament of Reconciliation or Penance is of great importance in restoring the sanctity and unity that we sinful human beings often damage by our thoughts, words, and deeds. Therefore the Holy Father teaches that "Repentance and mutual pardon within the bosom of the Christian family, so much a part of daily life, receive their specific sacramental expression in Christian Penance." In turn, life close to the sacraments builds the sacrament of Matrimony and the family into a spiritual structure that will endure all attacks. Such a life is your privilege and duty as a Catholic.

Simply put, prayer is nothing more than human conversation with God—both listening and talking. Though it need not be complicated, family prayer is an essential for maintaining the domestic Church, just as public prayer is essential for the larger Church. One can actually speak of the family as having a *liturgical life* parallel to and derived from the liturgical life of the Church. Indeed, unless the family literally derives its spiritual strength from the Sacrifice of the Mass and the sacrament of Reconciliation, it will not be a true domestic Church.

Family prayer is "prayer offered *in common*."[15] It is listening together to the word of God in the Bible, in sermons at Mass, and in spiritual writings. It is also addressing Him to express our needs and desires. Often, listening is the more important element. Those who come to the Church for marriage should form the habit of reading and reflecting on the Scriptures, the lives and writings of the saints, and writings of the Holy Father and others to whom Christ has given positions of responsibility and leadership. They should become accustomed *as a family* to address God with their needs, their upsets, their gratitude. Prayer time should also be a time of self-examination and of great honesty. After all, God does not deceive and cannot be deceived.

Read together. Pray together. Pray the Rosary together. Pray morning and evening prayer—or just one of these—from the Divine Office together. Lay use of the Divine Office is encouraged by the Second Vatican Council. Know when you do this that you will be praying with the faithful clergy and religious over the whole world, and so joining the voice of your domestic Church with that of the whole Church. Pray before, or before and after, meals. Express your gratitude not only for the food you eat and the place where you live, but for each other. Your sense of God's presence will increase quickly if you as a couple together thank Him for the mutual gift of your marriage. Pray when you begin and end a trip.

If you have any inhibitions about praying together, you will find that they disappear quickly once you get started. So start. Now. Even before you are married. Remember that you are God's gift to each other. Thank Him.

• *Education*

The Holy Father finds in the educational function of the family an extension of the prophetic role of Christ. It is a part of the general Christian vocation to bring the Christian perspective to every aspect of life. That is also what education in Christianity does inside the family. In the Christian family children learn to interpret their own lives and the elements of the culture around them in terms of God's word and the teaching of His Church. This keeps them spiritually aware and alive. This application of spiritual understanding to one's surroundings and one's own will is the essence of prophecy. It leads to *prudence*—to a wisdom that sees the present and the probable future in the light of eternity, and makes its choices accordingly. It leads the young to be "signs of contradiction" against social wrongs. Leaving aside the Scriptural function of the prophet as a seer of things to come, the habit of applying God's word to events around us and of living in accord with that word is the chief goal of a Christian education. Children can—and must—be taught this habit.

"The mission to educate," according to the Church, "demands that Christian parents should present to their children all the topics that are necessary for the gradual maturing of their personality from a Christian and ecclesial point of view."[16] As a couple desiring to be married in the Church, you will be asked, or have already been asked, if you are determined to raise your children in the faith. You must say Yes to this question. That is a natural requirement for a Catholic marriage, for the relation between the Church and the domestic Church is very close. The marriage is itself sacramental and blessed by the Church. The children born to that marriage are one chief good of your union (the other chief good being the union itself). The Church is vitally interested in them. They are therefore to be trained to "learn to adore God the Father in spirit and in truth . . . especially through liturgical worship."[17]

So a large part of educating children properly is teaching them to worship properly and take part vigorously in the life of the Church. *This is something that you as parents must plan to do: to get your children to Mass every Sunday and holy day right from the beginning, and to take an active role in guiding them through the sacraments of first Confession, first Communion, and Confirmation.*

Please don't just turn this job over to the Church. If you do, the result will be a failure. This is because you as parents are the "first heralds of the Gospel"[18] for your children. Regardless of what you do, they are going to learn more from you about how to live than from anyone else.

In addition to nurturing the children in the life of the Church, *the other great responsibility of Catholic parents is helping to form their consciences in accord with the moral law,* so that they can make upright decisions in accord with Christ's teaching. When they see you turn to the word of God and to the Church for answers to questions of right and wrong, they will learn that the Holy Spirit guides the Church in matters of morals as well as matters of faith. If, on the other hand, they learn from you the false teaching that right and wrong are a matter of individual decision, they will grow up without an understanding of reality. *Nothing* can substitute for your right living—no school, no Church, no "educational television," no Internet, no teacher. You have an essential educational function.

• *Service*

The educational function of the family leads naturally to its service function, which is parallel to the kingly role of Christ. The Church, of all human societies, is unique in being blessed with a King like ours. For Christ's entire mission was service. He came to serve. This is how He exercises His kingship. The whole course of His life was self-sacrifice. For His servants also, *service* is how to live in the Kingdom.

Catholic families, like Catholic individuals, are called to be the salt of the earth and the light of the world (Matthew 5.13,14). These images symbolize *service to mankind.* The family is not just turned in upon itself. Its members are not the only beneficiaries of its teaching. Indeed, in order to benefit truly from the Gospel, Christian children must learn to serve the genuine interests of their fellow man wherever those interests lie. The Catholic family therefore has a clear social function—to *serve others,* both through testimony and through example. Christian families are indispensable in working toward what the Holy Father calls the larger "civilization of love"[19] and the "culture of life."[20] It is your duty to form a family that will serve this end.

We see all around us the fearful results of family disunity and dysfunction. In this negative context, the task of the Catholic family is a positive one. It involves constructing a sacramental community of love out of reverence for Christ, and extending that community through the generations. But it also involves a negative role, for it must exclude moral disorders from itself. By its example, teaching, and rearing of Godly children, it must work toward eradicating these evils in the larger society.

In your study of Catholic teaching you may encounter the idea that society is "subsidiary" to the family. The subsidiarity of society to the family means that society should recognize the primary importance of the family as a social unit, and know that the very life of a nation comes from its families—not from government or universities or social projects. For this reason, the laws of a nation should serve the family and recognize its sovereignty. Only when the family is properly valued can it fulfill its own service role. I am afraid that as a nation we have greatly devalued the family and tried to make it subsidiary to everything else. As Catholics, however, you and I must move in the opposite direction—toward the recognition of the family as the basic social unit, and toward laws and customs that will encourage its health. Then it can fulfill its God-given role.

The family has a true "vocation" and "apostolate" in the world, both clarified by the teaching authority of the Church. According to Vatican II, raising a family is part of the normal "apostolate of the laity. Families are meant to contribute to the transformation of the earth and the renewal of the world, of creation and of all humanity."[21] The Church teaches that the quality of a nation's citizens is equal to that of its families. Married couples "give birth to children for the nation, so that they can be members of it and can share in its historic and cultural heritage."[22]

It is easy to see that this fact brings additional obligations. A Catholic couple shares in God's creation by having children and raising them not only in the service of the family, of God and His Church, and of the children's own wellbeing, but in the service of building a just and free society. We are only beginning to realize how socially destructive the modern breakdown of the family has been. *You as a Catholic couple are called to be a sign of contradic-*

tion to this breakdown.

Conflict resolution by the "commandment of Christ." Jesus gave very few commandments. He did teach that the Ten Commandments of the Old Testament are binding—commandments against adultery, theft, lying, coveting your neighbor's property, and so forth. He also taught a two-part epitome of the Old Testament:

> You shall love the Lord your God with all your heart, and with all your soul, and with all your mind. This is the great and first commandment. And a second is like it. You shall love your neighbor as yourself. On these two commandments depend all the law and the prophets (Matthew 22.37-40).

These great commandments, however, were not original at the time of Christ, but were His careful summation of the old law.

So what does Jesus refer to as His own commandment? Simply this: *"Love one another."* But He turns the old commandment to love our neighbor into something new. We must love each other *as Christ loved us.* Thus Jesus says, "A new commandment I give to you, that you love one another; *even as I have loved you,* that you also love one another" (John 13.34). The great challenge to those who would follow Christ is to *obey* this commandment without fail. Such obedience would make serious marital conflict obsolete.

But we are not perfect. As every adult knows, there is no marriage without conflict. For this reason, you need to have some agreement about how you will handle disputes. You shouldn't take the matter for granted. A few suggestions follow below. One thing is clear: conflicts that persist, that will not be resolved, always result from a failure to love. Love may be momentarily displaced by emotion, but we must return to it as the basis of our relationship.

Anger, for instance, comes over us before we know it. It sneaks up, we feel it rising and may even encourage it. Then we lash out at the person who causes it, or perhaps at someone who *doesn't* cause it—very often the person we love most in the world. The duty of a Catholic couple is to be aware of this danger. They must recognize that fury, though sometimes unavoidable, is dangerous to love.

Usually, marital conflict results from an excessive sensitivity. If you are in a bad mood and are determined to find insult in what someone else says or does, you will find it. If you are in a bad mood and are looking for ways to *give* insult, you will find them. One of the facts of marriage is that you will always know very well how to irritate each other—how to evoke an angry response. You should resolve right now that you will always avoid using this knowledge to "get" each other. Then you should try very hard to live by your resolution.

As Christians we are called to rise above our instincts. We are called to live as much as possible on the rational level, not the emotional or instinctual level. The rational soul, the part in us that comes from God and is created in His image, must control us. Remember that God's love for us is not an emotion. It is an act of His Will. Real love—our love itself—is also not an emotion, though our emotions are tied up with it. It is a deliberately chosen commitment to the welfare of the beloved person. An act of will. That is why it is so wrong to harbor anger, to try to keep it hot. To do so is deliberately to override the divine part of our nature so we can be ruled by a negative emotion. The desire to do this comes from Satan, and we should resist it to the best of our ability. Though they may feel good in a perverse way, continued anger and resentment are the opposite of forgiveness, and as such are gravely wrong. What's more, anger can destroy a marriage.

This book is not meant to substitute for counseling. If conflict lasts too long or seems to come from an intractable problem, you should get professional help from a marriage counselor. *If you do so, do your best to find a Catholic counselor who is loyal to the Church's teachings.* Many counselors have a false idea of marriage and of the world in general. If you choose one whose concepts come from Hollywood or from a school of thought that excludes God, counseling will probably do more harm than good. If you can't find a true Catholic marriage counselor, an evangelical Protestant would probably be next best. Just don't pick an atheist or some other kind of screwball. You need someone who understands human nature as it really is. A human being is a creature who partakes of God's nature, is under God's judgment, and has been given divine guidance on how to live. An atheist cannot give you reliable guidance here, since he doesn't know the most important fundamental truths about creation.

The chances are very good, however, that you will never have to see a professional counselor.

» Here is a prescription for the future. This is something
that I tell every couple in their wedding ceremony. When
conflict arises, stop and think and ask yourself if your
thoughts, words, and actions *at that moment* are in *complete* accord with the love that you express for each other
right now. If they aren't, they should be changed.

A few practical rules may be in order. These may be supple-
mented by numerous popular publications if necessary. (Just ask
in any large bookstore about works on "conflict resolution.")

• *First, resolve here and now that you will never cultivate
anger.* Learn to see anger as an emotion like its first cousins,
fear and self-pity. They all come together. Don't kid yourself that your anger is "justified." Let it go. Let your spouse
know that you want to resolve your conflict. Studies show
that the peace of mind you will arrive at will help you to
sleep better and even live longer. *In biblical terms: don't let
the sun go down on your anger* (Ephesians 4.26).

• *Second, no stonewalling.* Resolving not to talk to "that
creep" will only make matters worse. Deciding "I'll show
her. Hell will freeze over before I say another word to her"
will only damage *you* and the life *you* have chosen. It will
also overtax your adrenal system, postpone your own spiritual comfort, spoil your sleep, make you itch, and endanger
your marriage. Communication leads to reconciliation. Letting your guard down will restore your mutual caring and
tranquility. You are not getting married in order to wall each
other off. Remember that mutual caring is what your marriage is about. You have chosen it rationally. Maintain it in
the same way.

• *Third, be the first to say you are sorry.* You have heard that
"love means never having to say you're sorry." This idea
scores 100 percent for stupidity. It's an absolute nonstarter.
Jesus said, "Blessed are the peacemakers" (Matthew 5.9). If
you determine to be the peacemaker in your marriage, peace
will be made. If you determine to keep the conflict up, it
won't matter what your husband or wife does—the battle
will continue. Don't worry about whose "fault" the quarrel

is. In the best scenario, *we forgive others even as we are being wronged—even while the wrong is occurring. This especially applies to those we love.* Unfortunately, we like to show how fallen we are by taking every offense that's offered and getting hot about it. But a quarrel requires two people. Take it upon yourself to make peace.

• *Fourth, don't blame each other.* If your feelings are hurt, say "I feel hurt." Don't say, "You did this on purpose" or "That's what I expected from you" or some other accusation. *Talking about your feelings is all right. Talking about your spouse's motives or intentions is not.* Remember that most of the anger in the world—perhaps all of it—is a result of hurt feelings and self-pity. When we act angry, we are usually covering these feelings up. We try to get even by blame and accusations. This prolongs the strife. Somehow, Satan has taught us that there is more dignity or autonomy in being angry than in admitting we are hurt. But Satan is wrong. He is the father of lies.

• *Fifth, discuss conflict resolution coolly before you marry.* You already know what makes your fiancée mad. You know how to get her, and she knows how to get you. While you are planning your marriage, you should talk about this matter and promise each other that you will not deliberately irritate each other. You should also decide upon some "rules of engagement" by which you will handle disagreements. Those that I have named might actually be enough.

• *Sixth, study the Sacred Scripture's specifications about love and strive to live up to them.* The Holy Father teaches that the *"hymn to love* in the *First Letter to the Corinthians"* is the *"Magna Charta* of the civilization of love."[23]

> » *Here is that Great Charter, or Magna Charta, in full:*
> If I speak in the tongues of men and of angels, but have not love, I am a noisy gong or a clanging cymbal. And if I have prophetic powers, and understand all mysteries and all knowledge, and if I have all faith, so as to remove mountains, but have not love, I am nothing. If I give away all I have, and if I deliver my body to be burned, but have not love, I gain nothing.

Love is patient and kind; love is not jealous or boastful; it is not arrogant or rude. Love does not insist on its own way; it is not irritable or resentful; it does not rejoice at wrong, but rejoices in the right. Love bears all things, believes all things, hopes all things, endures all things.

Love never ends; as for prophecies, they will pass away; as for tongues, they will cease; as for knowledge, it will pass away. For our knowledge is imperfect and our prophecy is imperfect; but when the perfect comes, the imperfect will pass away. When I was a child, I spoke like a child, I thought like a child, I reasoned like a child; when I became a man, I gave up childish ways. For now we see in a mirror dimly, but then face to face. Now I know in part; then I shall understand fully, even as I have been fully understood. So faith, hope, love abide, these three; but the greatest of these is love (1 Corinthians 13).

Some observations on this famous and beautiful passage of Scripture:

• *Paragraph one teaches that eloquence, insight, spiritual power, and almsgiving are empty and worthless unless they are an expression of love.*

• *In beautiful and familiar language, paragraph two lists various positive and negative aspects of love.*

You should study these and reflect upon them, asking God to guide your thoughts and actions. Though the language is familiar and the passage is a favorite, the love described will demand real effort on your part. What does it mean, for instance, if love is patient? Is patience merely temporary tolerance of someone else's stupid opinion? If so, isn't it just about the same thing as *im*patience? Am I being patient if I insist on having things my way because to do so is my "right"? On the other hand, is patience the same thing as not having an opinion and not knowing how to express one's own mind? What does it mean to say that God is patient with us human beings?

Do I *really* have to give full attention to my wife's opinions, to accord full dignity to her experiences, to empathize with her feelings? Yes. God does this to us because He created us as *persons—*

shared His supreme personhood with us—and treats us as persons.
Please: give full, prayerful, long attention to the meaning of paragraph two of First Corinthians 13. Reread it often and meditate on
it.

• *The final paragraph affirms that love is eternal.*

Our faith in God will stop being faith when we see Him face to
face. It will turn into knowledge. At the same time, we will stop
hoping, for hope ends when its object is obtained. The pardoned
prisoner no longer hopes for his pardon. You won't hope for heaven
when you are there. But love is different. It is eternal. Inasmuch as
we love, we are like God, Who is eternal. Of these three "theological virtues"—faith, hope, and love—love is the one that lasts forever. Conflict will eventually pass away forever in the radiant presence of Love Himself.

Discussion questions

1. Why do you suppose people react with anger when their feelings are hurt? Is this reaction completely honest?
2. If love is an act of the will, why is it not something that you fall
into?
3. Who in your own experience has fulfilled the role of mother
best? Of father? How?
4. What kind of relationship would you like to have with your in-
laws?
5. Why did the Second Vatican Council call the family a "domestic
Church"?
6. What family values would you like to see in public or political
life?

Notes to Chapter 7

(1) Pope John Paul II, *Letter to Families*, no. 19 (Boston: Pauline Books & Media, 1994).

(2) Pope John Paul II, *Familiaris Consortio*, no. 25, in *Vatican Council II: More
Postconciliar Documents*, ed. Austin Flannery (Grand Rapids, Michigan:
Eerdmans, 1982). All quotations in this paragraph are from this passage.

(3) Loc. cit.

(4) *Catechism of the Catholic Church*, no. 400.

Journey of Faith:

(5) *Gaudium et Spes (Pastoral Constitution on the Church in the Modern World)*, no. 52, in *Vatican Council II: The Conciliar and Postconciliar Documents,* ed. Austin Flannery (Northport, New York: Costello, 1975).

(6) Loc. cit.

(7) Pope John Paul II, *Letter to Families*, no. 15.

(8) Ibid., no. 10.

(9) Pope John Paul II, *Familiaris Consortio*, no. 27.

(10) Vatican II, *Apostolicam Actuositatem*, no. 11, in Vatican II: *Conciliar and Postconciliar Documents*, ed. Austin Flannery (Northport, New York: Costello, 1975). Cf. *Letter to Families*, no. 19, and *Familiaris Consortio*, no 49. The Holy Father derived the phrase "domestic Church" from the Second Vatican Council. Every couple marrying in the Catholic Church should meditate on the resemblances between a loving family and the Church, and on how the Church and the family depend upon each other.

(11) Pope John Paul II, *Letter to Families*, no. 19.

(12) Pope John Paul II, *Familiaris Consortio*, no. 49.

(13) Ibid., no. 55. Italics in the original.

(14) Ibid., no. 58.

(15) Ibid., no. 59. Italics in the original.

(16) Ibid., no. 39.

(17) Ibid. The quotation includes an imbedded quotation from John 4.23.

(18) Ibid.

(19) *Letter to Families*. "The Civilization of Love" is the title of the central section.

(20) See Pope John Paul II, *Evangelium Vitae (The Gospel of Life)*, 1997.

(21) Pope John Paul II, *Letter to Families*, no. 18.

(22) Ibid., no. 17.

(23) Ibid., no. 14. Italics in original.

CHAPTER 8

MONEY AND POSSESSIONS

We live in an age that is probably unparalleled in history for its selfishness and materialism. Strangely enough, this is chiefly a middle-class phenomenon, for the Western middle class is the world's first class large enough and wealthy enough to live as we live and think as we think. Really wealthy people have always lived lavishly. Not until modern times, however, has such an immense middle class existed. This class—wealthy beyond the dreams of many people in the world—has been responsible for most of the advances of the Western world. From it come the taxes that run governments. From it come most of the leaders of the world. From the middle class come the overwhelming number of entrepreneurs, doctors, lawyers, teachers, clergymen, authors, and other outstanding individuals. The contributions of the middle class to human advancement, based on private property rights and relative economic freedom, have been great. They must not be underestimated. There is also nothing basically wrong with the economic activity that has led to such benefits.

Nevertheless, true Christianity has always been on guard against the allure of wealth as such. I believe that the warnings of the Scriptures and the Church are particularly important now. For we have now had more than two centuries of materialism since the Industrial Revolution. Materialism in two senses: 1) in the emphasis on getting money, and 2) in the emphasis on a materialistic philosophy. These two are connected but are not the same; the connection isn't essential. The second is far worse than the first. A materialistic philosophy asserts falsely that the universe is material only, that spirit doesn't exist, that man is just a mortal animal, that God is just a fiction. Mere money-grubbing, by contrast, is much less poisonous to the human spirit.

Most people in our culture—the vast middle class—don't claim to be materialistic in the second sense. The large majority claim to believe in God. But in spite of this, very many act as if materialistic philosophy were true. They forget that there is an eternal dimension to all human acts. Consequently, they commit all the sins

85

associated with the illusion that you can "have it all" and "have it now."

In marriage, the results of this materialism-in-action are divorce, contraception, abortion, strife, adultery, fornication, masturbation, and other loveless, self-serving evils. These result, of course, not directly from the desire for possessions but from the underlying false materialistic assumption that God doesn't see or care what we do. Combine this lie with the self-indulgence of the sexual revolution, and you arrive at the same result that materialism in the philosophical sense leads to. A disaster.

Stewardship and faith: Christian morality with regard to possessions. The misguided faith of materialists is dangerous to marriage. In your marriage, as in all of life, your money and possessions should be kept in proper perspective. If you want to follow Christ—and so receive the rewards that come from a life spent in His service—you have to have a Christian attitude toward money and possessions. In the Old Testament as well as the New, God's people have always understood the simple but profound truth that ultimate trust in *anything* besides God is a form of idolatry. Even if you put your spouse before God, for instance, that is worship of an idol. So much more so is the worship of money. And idolatry leads to death.

Let's face it. All of the old wisdom about the spiritual danger of living for money is true. It's not just empty preaching. That is why Jesus accepted and taught it—because He had insight into truths that exist in the nature of things. Some of these were revealed long before His birth on earth. As long before Christ as the Psalms, Hebrew poets and wise men had warned their audiences about the futility of trusting in riches:

> Be not afraid when one becomes rich,
> when the glory of his house increases.
> For when he dies he will carry nothing away;
> his glory will not go down after him (Psalm 49.16-17).

On many occasions Jesus takes up the theme. He teaches that "No servant can serve two masters; for either he will hate the one and love the other, or he will be devoted to the one and despise the other. You cannot serve God and mammon" (Luke 16. 13). "Mammon" means earthly possessions or money. Jesus teaches us, in fact, to dispose of our possessions so that we can give the proceeds to others in need:

> Sell your possessions, and give alms; provide yourselves with purses that do not grow old, with treasure in the heavens that does not fail, where no thief approaches and no moth destroys. For where your treasure is, there will your heart be also (Luke 12.32-34).

He teaches the great *spiritual* danger of money, even implying that most rich people will end up excluded from heaven because of their misplaced values:

> "How hard it is for those who have riches to enter the kingdom of God! For it is easier for a camel to go through the eye of a needle than for a rich man to enter the kingdom of God." Those who heard it said, "Then who can be saved?" But He said, "What is impossible with men is possible with God" (Luke 18.24-27).

Some teachers claim that the Lord was referring to a place called the "Needle's Eye," where a camel could just squeeze through. Thus they make null the real point. Jesus is in fact teaching that *almost everyone who succeeds in obtaining wealth is going to put that wealth before God and fail to reach God's eternal kingdom.*

So do you have to *plan* to be poor? Are you forbidden to work for money? No, definitely not. The Church has always depended upon materially successful people for help. Society has also profited greatly from the cultural monuments made possible because someone was wealthy. The fine medieval museum in Upper Manhattan known as the Cloisters, for instance, was a gift from one of the Rockefellers. Thousands have been enriched by it.

St. Paul leads us toward the *balance* required by the Church's teaching:

> As for the rich in this world, charge them not to be haughty, nor to set their hopes on uncertain riches but on God Who richly furnishes us with everything to enjoy. They are to do good, to be rich in good deeds, liberal and generous, thus laying up for themselves a good foundation for the future, so that they may take hold of the life which is life indeed (First Timothy 6.17-19).

To St. Paul, then, wealth is good as long as it doesn't make its possessors act superior. He teaches us not to "set our hopes" on it. We must *use it generously for the benefit of others.*

That leads to one of the most important concepts about how followers of Christ are to conduct themselves.

> » We are to live as stewards of God's gifts, knowing that we came into the world with nothing and will take nothing out of it.

Job, the servant of God, states the matter: "Naked I came from my mother's womb, and naked shall I return" (Job 1.21). *Stewardship* is the function of using something that actually belongs to someone else in a wise and responsible way. We are to use all that we have, which is given to us by God, for the benefit of God's kingdom. The beautiful part is that our whole lives can be the exercise of stewardship, no matter what our vocation.

The things we own really belong to us, though we must ultimately leave them, for property ownership is a necessity for stewardship. You can't be responsible for something that isn't *yours*. In the idea of Christian stewardship is the knowledge that God really lets us own things so that we can prove to be responsible in our use of them.

This concept is included in St. Paul's statements about generosity. It is also included in Christ's admonition to "give alms," for giving to the poor is a *necessary* part of Christian stewardship. You should know for certain that possessions and money are less important than your spouse and your marriage. They are also less important than the lives and wellbeing of the poor.

One of the temptations to which young married couples are especially subject in these days of immoral birth-control measures is the temptation to postpone having children until the family is financially secure. We read repeatedly about women who have avoided pregnancy until they are practically middle-aged, only to find out with great regret that they have spent the best part of their lives in the wrong pursuit—the quest for money and career. Such broken-hearted women make the news with some regularity. Money and career are fine, but you should know which is more important. Bringing children into the world and raising them in the Body of Christ is a task of lasting value, whereas being a corporate board member or successful professional is an empty goal unless it is subordinated to something more important. The Holy Father writes that those who are

> imprisoned in a consumer mentality and whose sole concern is to bring about a continual growth of material goods, finish by ceasing to understand, and thus by refusing, the spiritual riches of a new human life. The ultimate reason for these mentalities is the absence in people's hearts of God, whose love alone is stronger than all the world's fears and can conquer them.[1]

Letting your fears of financial insecurity control you is a failure of faith. True, thoughtfulness in planning for a child is wise. Getting a handle on finances for the future is important. But if you're like most people, real financial security may come very late in your life or not at all. Most people arrive at Social Security age with *no* money saved. *None.* Needless to say, many of these people have successfully raised children. They have often led richer lives than wealthy people, who tend to have more divorces and family strife. God will help you if you're willing to trust Him and go ahead with starting your family. And you should always remember that Jesus Himself didn't have much of a portfolio.

Almsgiving. Jesus requires those who would be His followers to "sell all they have and give to the poor." Certainly we cannot hope to please God unless our entire lives are subordinated to the Gospel. In this sense, even the successful businessman gives all he has to Christ—by doing everything in the Lord's name. Jesus didn't mean that it is wrong to make a living. He did mean that our whole lives have to be given to knowing and following God's will. For the vast majority of people, this includes pursuing the vocation of married life. In this life fiscal responsibility and financial self-sufficiency are of great value.

Still, giving alms is not optional. You are *required* to support your parish and to express your concern for the poor in gifts that will help them. Sometimes this means giving time or labor instead of money. But giving there must be. If you are able, you are also responsible for supporting such Godly causes as the pro-life movement. In this era of mass communications, money doesn't go very far, and those who are publicly fighting the Lord's battles need your support, both in effort and in money.

How much should you give? A basic rule might be: if you are perfectly comfortable, if you don't notice any sacrifice in your charities, you probably aren't giving enough away. Remember the widow in the New Testament who gave her last two small coins to the temple and was praised by Jesus (Mark 12.41-44). She gave what she needed for herself, not just something that happened to be left over. There are no binding rules on the matter except this: you must *plan* thoughtfully and sincerely to give a reasonable amount of your income to "the Lord"—that is, to the Church and to charitable causes. To fail to do so is seriously sinful.

St. Paul says that the person who has plenty should be willing to share with those in need, and the favor will be returned if necessity arises. Jesus teaches clearly that the Works of Mercy performed for the "least of [his] brothers" are performed for Him (Matthew 25.40) and will receive a just reward. About this reward St. Paul speaks:

> The point is this: he who sows sparingly will also reap sparingly, and he who sows bountifully will also reap bountifully. Each one must do as he has made up his mind, not reluctantly or under compulsion, for God loves a cheerful giver (2 Corinthians 9.6-7).

Plan your family budget so as to do your duty in supporting the Church and helping those in need. Remember that if you live in Europe or America, you are rich by comparison with billions of other people. Help them.

Budget planning. Notice the word *planning.* Don't let your financial life occur without forethought. That can lead to disaster. *Be aware that money problems are involved in most divorces.* They may not be the only factor, but they are almost always there. *Do not fail to talk over your financial plans before you marry.* Discuss your financial habits—how you pay bills, what risks you are willing to take, the relative importance of money to you, your possible inclination to "blow it off" whether you can afford to or not. You may discover that one of you has a lifelong habit of taking money matters for granted, or a presumption that someone else is responsible, or even a habit of reckless spending and wastefulness.

If you find out that your future spouse doesn't want to talk about it, so much the worse. These are the elements of future strife, and they cannot safely be ignored. What's more, if both of you make good salaries before marriage and expect to do so afterward, that fact does not exempt you from planning. It may, in fact, make planning *more* imperative, since a habit of prosperity may have led to real carelessness about the future. If one of you is genuinely well off, that fact may in itself be a spiritual danger. If one of you has been pampered and spoiled and the other has worked for a living for years, you must come to terms with this difference or it will cause trouble. What terms? You should remember that St. Paul said anyone who wouldn't work shouldn't be allowed to eat (2 Thessalonians 3.10).

This book doesn't pretend to tell you what kind of budget to make, only that you should make one. Plan how much you will spend, and on what, in accord with how much you make. Lay out your projected expenses beside your projected income. Give yourselves an allowance out of the difference and save the rest. Don't wait to begin saving for your retirement; it will come sooner than you dream. As I have said, most people are not ready for it.

Plan not to live beyond your means. This requires, for one thing, that you shun casual credit. This applies especially to high-interest credit such as that obtained with credit cards. Avoid these as you would avoid a scorpion. The very fact of *needing* credit often indicates a desire for what one can't afford. Of course, the decision to buy something considered necessary on credit—a car or a house or an expensive appliance—may be perfectly rational. Also, if you need credit for a genuine investment in the future, such as education, borrowing is often justified. Be forewarned, however, that paying back student loans is a long-term and dreary project. You may choose to borrow anyway. But to use credit cards for routine expenses is irrational—and it will get you into trouble.

If you have a lot of money, you should ask yourself about the morality of living in mansions and driving super-expensive cars when some people in the world are starving.

Much financial software is available to help make a budget. You will also find many books on personal finance at any good bookstore. Why not have a look at them? And—apropos of the next chapter—remember that the most important part of your wedding ceremony is the *least* expensive part.

Discussion questions

1. What money responsibilities did you have as a child? What money responsibilities do you have now? Do you need to change?
2. When the widow in the Gospel gave away her last two cents, who profited and why?
3. Read the story of the rich man and Lazarus, Luke 16.19-31. Why do you suppose the rich man went to hell?
4. Suppose you wanted a house you couldn't afford, and you worked two jobs to get it. But you sacrificed your home life and your marriage in the process. How much did it really cost? Would you own it, or would it own you?

Note to Chapter 8

(1) Pope John Paul II, *Familiaris Consortio*, no. 30, in *Vatican Council II: More Postconciliar Documents*, ed. Austin Flannery (Grand Rapids, Michigan: Eerdmans, 1982).

CHAPTER 9

PLANNING YOUR CEREMONY

Some of your choices. Much of what happens at your wedding depends upon your own choices. Every diocese and most parishes have some rules in addition to the general requirements of the Church. Some, for instance, allow no flash photography during the wedding. Others may specify what kind of decorations, including flowers, you may use. Music especially is the subject of regulations: nothing inappropriate for the occasion or holy setting should be used. Many churches also charge a fee for weddings. You should understand that this is not "selling the sacraments." It is, rather, a necessity imposed by the fact that the Church exists in the economic world. Costs for electricity, property taxes, cleaning, maintenance, and other needs are a fact of life. If you want to get married in a particularly attractive church where you are not parishioners, you will probably be charged more. This is because, unlike parishioners, you are not already contributing to the upkeep of the parish.

The wedding ceremony offers you the *unfortunate* opportunity of spending vast amounts of money. Among other extravagances you can pay thousands of dollars for musicians, flowers, clothes, limousines, food, drink, rented furniture, rented party space, guests' airline tickets, and, of course, the honeymoon. The sky's the limit. You can also impose on your relatives and friends to buy you thousands of dollars worth of gifts. This may, however, result in a situation *where no one present understands what is really going on.* I strongly urge you not to do this, but to consider what is truly important in your wedding—your public commitment to each other and to Christ to enter a permanent sacramental union. If you are not careful, these other considerations will distract you from the real significance of the event. The trivia will absorb all your attention. Don't let this happen.

A Catholic wedding usually takes place within Mass. This is the ideal setting for it. If, however, you want to marry outside of Mass, the Church allows it. In fact, marriage without Mass is the norm for unions between Catholics and baptized members of other Christian communions. This is so since the inability of non-Catholics to receive Communion can cause awkwardness.

Remember that the Catholic Church does not offer Communion to non-Catholics, even to non-Catholic brides or grooms. This is not to exclude them, but only to acknowledge and honor the reality that complete union between the Catholic Church and non-Catholic Christian bodies, sadly, doesn't exist. The lack of union is not only formal, however. It also extends to belief. Most non-Catholics don't have the same *faith* about the Eucharist that Catholics have. When a Protestant receives Communion, he is usually not doing the same thing a Catholic does, for Catholics believe they are receiving the true Body and Blood of Christ, not merely symbolic bread and wine. In other words, "intercommunion" presupposes a unity of faith and practice that does not exist. Nevertheless, with the bishop's permission, a mixed marriage may take place within Mass.

Whether your wedding occurs within the context of the Mass or not, most of your choices are the same. You can choose readings (and usually readers), prayers, music, and other elements of the ceremony. Some local and ethnic elements may be used. I particularly like the *lazo* ceremony, which many Hispanics use as a part of their wedding. In this custom, the kneeling couple are linked together by a large rosary. The presence and prayers of the Blessed Virgin are thereby clearly invoked, and the couple are encouraged to live their life close to her. The *unity candle* is likewise an effective symbol of the marital union and the presence of God. If these or other wedding customs appeal to you, chances are your clergyman will be happy to include them.

The Liturgy of the Word

The Liturgy of the Word in a wedding Mass employs the same pattern of readings as that in any other Mass—an Old Testament reading, a responsorial psalm, a New Testament reading, and a Gospel reading. The readings that follow are *selected* from the wedding section of the *Lectionary*, the official Catholic book of Mass readings. They are my favorites. Although they are good readings, they are not the only possible ones. If you have a favorite Bible reading, ask your priest or deacon if he will allow you to substitute it for one of these. You will need to select one from each section. Getting friends or relatives to be readers is usually encouraged. Remember, however, that the priest or deacon must read the Gospel.

Readings

Old Testament

1. Genesis 1.26-28, 31
A reading from the book of Genesis

God said: "Let us make man in our image, after our likeness. Let them have dominion over the fish of the sea, the birds of the air, and the cattle, and over all the wild animals and all the creatures that crawl on the ground."

God created man in His image; in the divine image He created him; male and female He created them.

God blessed them, saying: "Be fertile and multiply; fill the earth and subdue it. Have dominion over the fish of the sea, the birds of the air, and all the living things that move on the earth." God looked at everything He had made, and He found it very good.

The Word of the Lord

2. Genesis 2.18-24
A reading from the book of Genesis

The Lord God said: "It is not good for the man to be alone. I will make a suitable partner for him." So the Lord God formed out of the ground various wild animals and various birds of the air, and He brought them to the man to see what he would call them; whatever the man called each of them would be its name. The man gave names to all the cattle, all the birds of the air, and all the wild animals; but none proved to be the suitable partner for the man.

So the Lord God cast a deep sleep on the man, and while he was asleep, he took out one of his ribs and closed up its place with flesh. The Lord God then built up into a woman the rib that He had taken from the man. When He brought her to the man, the man said,

"This one, at last is bone of my bones and flesh of my flesh;
This one shall be called 'woman,' for out of 'her man' this one has been taken."
That is why a man leaves his father and mother and clings to his wife, and the two of them become one body.

The Word of the Lord

3. Song of Songs 2.8-10, 14, 16; 8.6-7
A reading from the Song of Songs
Hark! my lover—here he comes
springing across the mountains,
leaping across the hills.
My lover is like a gazelle
or a young stag.
Here he stand behind our wall,
gazing through the windows,
peering through the lattices.
My lover speaks; he says to me,
"Arise, my beloved, my beautiful one, and come!
O my dove in the clefts of the rock,
in the secret recesses of the cliff,
Let me see you,
let me hear your voice,
For your voice is sweet, and you are lovely."
My lover belongs to me and I to him.
[He said to me:]
Set me as a seal on your heart,
as a seal on your arm;
For stern as death is love,
relentless as the nether world is devotion;
its flames are a blazing fire.
Deep waters cannot quench love,
nor floods sweep it away.

The Word of the Lord.

4. Sirach 26.1-4, 13-16
A reading from the book of Sirach

> Happy the husband of a good wife,
>> twice-lengthened are his days;
> A worthy wife brings joy to her husband;
>> peaceful and full is his life.
> A good wife is a generous gift
>> bestowed upon him who fears the Lord;
> Be he rich or poor, his heart is content
>> and a smile is ever on his face.
> A gracious wife delights her husband,
>> her thoughtfulness puts flesh on his bones;
> A gift from the Lord is her governed speech,
>> and her firm virtue is of surpassing worth.
> Choicest of blessings is a modest wife,
>> priceless her chaste person.
> Like the sun rising in the Lord's heavens,
>> the beauty of a virtuous wife is the radiance of her home.

The Word of the Lord

5. Jeremiah 31.31-32, 33-34
A reading from the book of Jeremiah

The days are coming, says the Lord, when I will make a new covenant with the house of Israel and the house of Judea. It will not be like the covenant I made with their fathers the day I took them by the hand to lead them forth from the land of Egypt. But this is the covenant I will make with the house of Israel after those days, says the Lord. I will place my law within them, and write it upon their hearts; I will be their God, and they shall be my people. No longer will they have need to teach their friends and kinsmen how to know the Lord. All, from least to greatest, shall know me, says the Lord.

The Word of the Lord

Journey of Faith:

Responsorial Psalm

1. From Psalm 34
Response: I will bless the Lord at all times.
I will bless the Lord at all times;
   his praise shall be ever in my mouth.
Let my soul glory in the Lord;
   the lowly will hear me and be glad.
Response: I will bless the Lord at all times.
Glorify the Lord with me,
   let us together extol his name.
I sought the Lord, and He answered me
   and delivered me from all my fears.
Response: I will bless the Lord at all times.
Look to Him that you may be radiant with joy
   and your faces may not blush with shame.
When the afflicted man called out, the Lord heard,
   and from all his distress He saved him.
Response: I will bless the Lord at all times.
The angel of the Lord encamps
   around those who fear him, and delivers them.
Taste and see how good the Lord is;
   happy the man who takes refuge in him.
Response: *I will bless the Lord at all times.*

2. From Psalm 128
Response: Happy are those who fear the Lord.
Happy are you who fear the Lord,
   who walk in His ways!
For you shall eat the fruit of your handiwork;
   happy shall you be, and favored.
Response: Happy are those who fear the Lord.
Your wife shall be like a fruitful vine
   in the recesses of your home;
Your children like olive plants
around your table.
Response: Happy are those who fear the Lord.
Behold, thus is the man blessed
who fears the Lord.
The Lord bless you from Sion:

may you see the prosperity of Jerusalem
all the days of your life.
Response: Happy are those who fear the Lord.

3. From Psalm 145
    Response: The Lord is compassionate to all His creatures.
    The Lord is gracious and merciful,
      slow to anger and of great kindness.
    The Lord is good to all
      and compassionate toward all His works.
    Response: The Lord is compassionate to all His creatures.
    Let all your works give you thanks, O Lord,
      and let your faithful ones bless you.
    The eyes of all look hopefully to you,
      and you give them their food in due season.
    Response: The Lord is compassionate to all His creatures.
    The Lord is just in all His ways
      and holy in all His works.
    The Lord is near to all who call upon him,
      to all who call upon Him in truth.
    Response: The Lord is compassionate to all His creatures.

4. From Psalm 148
    Response: Let all praise the name of the Lord.
    Praise the Lord from the heavens,
      praise Him in the heights;
    Praise him, all you His angels,
      praise him, all you His hosts.
    Response: Let all praise the name of the Lord.
    Praise him, sun and moon;
      praise him, all you shining stars.
    Praise him, you highest heavens,
      and you waters above the heavens.
    Response: Let all praise the name of the Lord.
    You mountains and all you hills,
      you fruit trees and all you cedars;
    You wild beasts and all tame animals,
      you creeping things and you winged fowl.
    Response: Let all praise the name of the Lord.

Let the kings of the earth and all peoples,
  the princes and all the judges of the earth,
Young men too, and maidens,
  old men and boys.
Response: Let all praise the name of the Lord.
Praise the name of the Lord,
  for His name alone is exalted;
His majesty is above earth and heaven,
  and He has lifted up the horn of His people.
Response: Let all praise the name of the Lord.

New Testament

1. Romans 8.31-35, 37-39

A reading from the letter of St. Paul to the Romans

If God is for us, who can be against us? Is it possible that He Who did not spare His own Son but handed Him over for the sake of us all will not grant us all things besides? Who shall bring a charge against God's chosen ones? God, Who justifies? Who shall condemn them? Christ Jesus, Who died or rather was raised up, Who is at the right hand of God and Who intercedes for us?

Who will separate us from the love of Christ? Trial, or distress, or persecution, or hunger, or nakedness, or the sword? Yet in all this we are more than conquerors because of Him Who has loved us. For I am certain that neither death nor life, neither angels nor principalities, neither the present nor the future, nor powers, neither height nor depth nor any other creature, will be able to separate us from the love of God that comes to us in Christ Jesus, our Lord.

The Word of the Lord

2. Romans 12.1-2, 9-13

A reading from the letter of St. Paul to the Romans

Brothers and sisters, I beg you through the mercy of God to offer your bodies as a living sacrifice holy and acceptable to God, your spiritual worship. Do not conform yourselves to this age but be transformed by the renewal of your mind so that you may judge what is God's will, what is good, pleasing and perfect.

Your love must be sincere. Detest what is evil, cling to what is good. Love one another with the affection of brothers. Anticipate each other in showing respect. Do not grow slack but be fervent in spirit; He Whom you serve is the Lord. Rejoice in hope, be patient under trial, persevere in prayer. Look on the need of the saints as your own; be generous in offering hospitality. The Word of the Lord

3. First Corinthians 12.31-13.8

A reading from the first letter of St. Paul to the Corinthians

Set your hearts on the greater gifts. I will show you the way which surpasses all the others. If I speak with human tongues and angelic as well, but do not have love, I am a noisy gong, a clanging cymbal. If I have the gift of prophecy and, with full knowledge, comprehend all mysteries, if I have faith great enough to move mountains, but have not love, I am nothing. If I give everything I have to feed the poor and hand over my body to be burned, but have not love, I gain nothing.

Love is patient; love is kind. Love is not jealous, it does not put on airs, it is not snobbish. Love is never rude, it is not self-seeking, it is not prone to anger; neither does it brood over injuries. Love does not rejoice in what is wrong but rejoices with the truth. There is no limit to love's forbearance, to its trust, its hope, its power to endure.

Love never fails.   The Word of the Lord

4. Ephesians 5.2, 21-33

A reading from the letter of St. Paul to the Ephesians

Follow the way of love, even as Christ loved you. He gave Himself for us.

Defer to one another out of reverence for Christ.

Wives should be submissive to their husbands as if to the Lord because the husband is head of his wife just as Christ is head of the Church, as well as its savior. As the Church submits to Christ, so wives should submit to their husbands in everything.

Husbands, love your wives, as Christ loved the Church. He gave Himself up for her to make her holy, purifying her in the bath of water by the power of the word, to present to Himself a glorious Church, holy and immaculate, without stain or wrinkle or anything of that sort. Husbands should love their wives as they do their own bodies. He who loves his wife loves himself. Observe that no one ever hates his own flesh; no, he nourishes it and takes care of it as Christ cares for the Church—for we are members of His body.

"For this reason a man shall leave his father and mother,
and shall cling to his wife,
and the two shall be made into one."

This is a great foreshadowing; I mean that it refers to Christ and the Church. In any case, each one should love his wife as he loves himself, the wife for her part showing respect for her husband. The Word of the Lord

5. Colossians 3.12-17

A reading from the letter of St. Paul to the Colossians

Because you are God's chosen ones, holy and beloved, clothe yourselves with heartfelt mercy, with kindness, humility, meekness, and patience. Bear with one another; forgive whatever grievances you have against one another. Forgive as the Lord has forgiven you. Over all these virtues put on love, which binds the rest together and makes them perfect. Christ's peace must reign in your hearts, since as members of the one body you have been called to that peace. Dedicate yourselves to thankfulness. Let the word of Christ, rich as it is, dwell in you. In wisdom made perfect, instruct and admonish one another. Sing gratefully to God from your hearts in psalms, hymns, and inspired songs. Whatever you do, whether in speech or in action, do it in the name of the Lord Jesus. Give thanks to God the Father through him. The Word of the Lord

6. 1 John 4.7-12

A reading from the first letter of St. John

Beloved,
let us love one another
because love is of God;
everyone who loves is begotten of God

and has knowledge of God.
The man without love has known nothing of God,
for God is love.
God's love was revealed in our midst in this way:
he sent His only Son to the world
that we might have life through him.
Love, then, consists in this:
not that we have loved God, but that He has loved us
and has sent His Son as an offering for our sins.
Beloved,
if God has loved us so,
we must have the same love for one another.
No one has ever seen God.
Yet if we love one another
God dwells in us,
and His love is brought to perfection in us.

The Word of the Lord

Gospel

1. Matthew 19.3-6

A reading from the Holy Gospel according to St. Matthew
Some Pharisees came up to Jesus and said, to test him, "May a man divorce his wife for any reason whatever?" He replied, "Have you not read that at the beginning the Creator made them male and female and declared, 'For this reason a man shall leave his father and mother and cling to his wife, and the two shall become as one'? Thus they are no longer two but one flesh. Therefore, let no man separate what God has joined."

The Gospel of the Lord

2. Mark 10.6-9

A reading from the Holy Gospel according to St. Mark
Jesus said: "At the beginning of creation God made them male and female; for this reason a man shall leave his father and mother and the two shall become as one. They are no longer two but one flesh. Therefore let no man separate what God has joined." The Gospel of the Lord

3. John 15.9-12

A reading from the Holy Gospel according to St. John
Jesus said to His disciples:
"As the father has loved me,
so I have loved you.
Live on in my love.
You will live in my love
if you keep my commandments,
even as I have kept my Father's commandments,
and live in His love.
All this I tell you
that my joy may be yours
and your joy may be complete.
This is my commandment:
love one another
as I have loved you."   The Gospel of the Lord

4. John 17.20-23

A reading from the Holy Gospel according to John
Jesus looked up to heaven and prayed:
"Holy Father,
I do not pray for my disciples alone.
I pray also for those who will believe in me through their
word,
that all may be one
as you, Father, are in me, and I in you;
I pray that they may be one in us,
that the world may believe that you sent me.
I have given them the glory you gave me
that they may be one, as we are one—
I living in them, you living in me—
that their unity may be complete.
So shall the world know that you sent me,
and that you love them as you loved me."
The Gospel of the Lord

THE RITE OF MARRIAGE: FORMS AND PRAYERS

The following forms and prayers come from the official Catholic book of rites and from the *Sacramentary*, the book the priest uses at the altar. In most cases they are selected from a range of choices. They have been chosen because they clearly reflect the principal themes of this book, and consequently the principal traits of Catholic marriage. The prayers and forms printed here are to be used when both parties to the marriage are Catholic or when the marriage is between a Catholic and a person baptized in another Christian communion. If the marriage is between a Catholic and a nonbaptized person, the forms are slightly different. Your priest or deacon will explain the differences.

From now on, I will assume that a priest is officiating.

Introductory Rite

The priest and the wedding party process to the altar and take their places. The entrance rite of Mass is followed by the first parts of the Liturgy of the Word—i.e., the readings you have chosen and the homily.

Then the priest addresses the couple:

My dear friends, you have come together in this church so that the Lord may seal and strengthen your love in the presence of the Church's minister and this community. Christ abundantly blesses this love. He has already consecrated you in Baptism and now He enriches and strengthens you by a special sacrament so that you may assume the duties of marriage in mutual and lasting fidelity. And so, in the presence of the Church, I ask you to state your intentions.

Questions

Priest:

N. and N., have you come here freely and without reservation to give yourselves to each other in marriage? (Each answers the questions separately.)

Will you love and honor each other as man and wife for the rest of your lives?

Will you accept children lovingly from God, and bring them up according to the law of Christ and His Church?

Consent (Vows)

Priest:

Since it is your intention to enter into marriage, join your right hands and declare your consent before God and His Church.

Bridegroom (repeating after the priest):

I, N., take you, N., to be my wife. I promise to be true to you in good times and in bad, in sickness and in health. I will love you and honor you all the days of my life.

Bride (repeating after the priest):

I, N., take you, N., to be my husband. I promise to be true to you in good times and in bad, in sickness and in health. I will love you and honor you all the days of my life.

Another form of consent

Bridegroom (repeating after the priest):

I, N., take you, N., for my lawful wife, to have and to hold, from this day forward, for better, for worse, for richer, for poorer, in sickness and in health, until death do us part.

Bride (repeating after the priest):

I, N., take you, N., for my lawful husband, to have and to hold, from this day forward, for better, for worse, for richer, for poorer, in sickness and in health, until death do us part.

Priest:

You have declared your consent before the Church. May the Lord in His goodness strengthen your consent and fill you both with His blessings. What God has joined, men must not divide.

Response Amen.

Blessing of rings

Priest:

May the Lord bless these rings which you give to each other as a sign of His love and fidelity.

Response Amen.

Exchange of rings

Bridegroom (placing his wife's ring on her finger):

N., take this ring as a sign of my love and fidelity. In the name of the Father, and of the Son, and of the Holy Spirit.

Bride (placing her husband's ring on his finger):

N., take this ring as a sign of my love and fidelity. In the name of the Father, and of the Son, and of the Holy Spirit.

» Now follow the general intercessions and Creed (as usual at Mass) and the Liturgy of the Eucharist.

» If the wedding takes place outside of Mass, the ceremony skips from the general intercessions to the nuptial blessing.

Nuptial blessing

Priest: Let us pray to the Lord for N. and N., who come to God's altar at the beginning of their married life, that they may always be united in love for each other (as now they share in the body and blood of Christ).

All pray silently for a short while. Then the priest extends his hands and continues:

Holy Father, you created mankind in your own image and made man and woman to be joined as husband and wife in union of body and heart and so fulfill their mission in this world.

Father, to reveal the plan of your love, you made the union of husband and wife an image of the covenant between you and your people. In the fulfillment of this sacrament, the marriage of Christian man and woman is a sign of the marriage between Christ and the Church.

Father, stretch out your hand and bless N. and N.

Lord, grant that as they begin to live this sacrament they may share with each other the gifts of your love and become one in heart and mind as witnesses to your presence in their marriage. Help them to create a home together and give them children to be formed by the Gospel and to have a place in your family.

Give your blessings to N., your daughter, so that she may be a good wife and mother, caring for the home, faithful in love for her husband, generous and kind.

Give your blessings to N., your son, so that he may be a faithful husband and a good father.

Father, grant that as they come together to your table on earth, so they may one day have the joy of sharing your feast in heaven.

We ask this through Christ our Lord. Amen.

Journey of Faith:

Solemn Blessing

Priest:
May God, the almighty Father, give you His joy and bless you in your children.
Response Amen.
May the only son of God have mercy on you and help you in good times and in bad.
Response Amen.
May the Holy Spirit of God always fill your hearts with His love.
Response Amen.
And may almighty God bless you all, the Father, and the Son, and the Holy Spirit.
Response Amen.
The recessional follows

SOURCES AND SUGGESTIONS
FOR FURTHER READING

The bibliography for marriage preparation, with all the subjects that it includes, is huge. All that is listed here is a few of the sources for this book and a few other recommended works. I strongly encourage you to read some of these books. I have put works of the Magisterium—the teaching Church—first. The editions of such works cited are convenient ones. They are not the only ones available. You can get almost any Church document from a good Catholic bookstore or from the Internet. Try:

www.vatican.va

You will find, however, that many Church documents are a bit long for downloading and printing. The following old-fashioned books may help.

Works of Pope John Paul II:
1. *Evangelium Vitae (The Gospel of Life)*. 1997. Defines the "culture of life" and its mortal opponent, the "culture of death." Vital for an understanding of current moral issues.

2. *Familiaris Consortio. From Vatican Council II: More Post Conciliar Documents*, ed. Austin Flannery. Grand Rapids, Michigan: Wm. B. Eerdmans Publishing Co., 1982. Profound and humble guidance for families seeking to live by God's law.

3. *Letter to Families*. Boston: St. Paul Books & Media, 1994. More of the same.

4. *Love and Responsibility.* New York: Farrar, Straus and Giroux, 1981. The nature and responsibility of human persons in truly loving relationships.

5. *The Theology of the Body.* Boston: Pauline Books & Media, 1997. To date, the ultimate exploration of the meaning of human sexuality. Difficult to read, but immensely rewarding.

6. *Veritatis Splendor (The Splendor of Truth)*. Boston: St. Paul Books

& Media, 1993. Defends the idea that truth exists, is glorious, and is accessible to those who seek it.

Documents of Vatican II:
Vatican Council II: The Conciliar and Post Conciliar Documents, ed. Austin Flannery. Northport, New York: Costello, 1975. See especially *Apostolicam Actuositatem (Decree on the Apostolate of Lay People)* and *Gaudium et Spes (Pastoral Constitution on the Church in the Modern World).*

Pope Paul VI.
Humanae Vitae (Of Human Life). 1968. Widely available. Also conveniently reprinted in the appendix to *The Theology of the Body,* above. The key text in the modern controversy about human sexuality.

Important other works:
Billings, Evelyn, and Ann Westmore. *The Billings Method: Controlling Fertility without Drugs or Devices.* New York: Ballantine, 1983. One of the "ovulation methods" of natural family planning.

Bonacci, Mary Beth. *Real Love.* San Francisco: Ignatius Press, 1996. A great book, readable, practical, and filled with insight. Every unmarried person should read this book.

Gerke, Leonard F. *Christian Marriage: A Permanent Sacrament.* Washington: Catholic University of America Press, 1965. The title says it all.

Grisez, Germain. *The Way of the Lord Jesus.* Volume 1: *Christian Moral Principles.* Chicago: Franciscan Herald Press, 1983. Volume 2: *Living a Christian Life.* Quincy, Illinois: Franciscan Press, 1993. Volume 3: *Difficult Moral Questions.* Quincy, Illinois: Franciscan Press, 1997. The great work of a leading moral theologian. Includes much discussion of marriage and morality.

Hilgers, Thomas W. *The Medical Applications of Natural Family Planning: A Contemporary Approach to Women's Health Care.*

Omaha, Nebraska: Pope Paul VI Institute Press, 1991. The "Creighton Method" of natural family planning: another of the "ovulation methods." Highly effective and highly recommended.

Kippley, John and Sheila. *The Art of Natural Family Planning.* Fourth edition. Cincinnati, Ohio: Couple to Couple League International, 1997. The "symptothermal method" of natural family planning. Widely used and respected.

Lewis, C. S. *The Four Loves.* New York: Harcourt, Brace and World, 1960. A classic on love by a Protestant theologian.

May, William E. *Marriage: The Rock on Which the Family Is Built.* San Francisco: Ignatius Press, 1995. A compressed theology of marriage.

Pieper, Joseph. *Faith, Hope, Love.* San Francisco: Ignatius Press, 1997. Philosophical discussions of the terms in the title. Highly recommended.